Appetizers

Appetizers

More than 70 deliciously
simple sharing plates and small
dishes to enjoy with friends

RYLAND PETERS & SMALL
LONDON • NEW YORK

Editor Lesley Malkin
Production Controller Sarah Kulasek-Boyd
Art Director Leslie Harrington
Editorial Director Julia Charles
Publisher Cindy Richards

Indexer Vanessa Bird

First published in 2016 by
Ryland Peters & Small
20–21 Jockey's Fields
London WC1R 4BW
and
341 E 116th St
New York NY 10029

www.rylandpeters.com

Recipe collection compiled by Julia Charles
Text © Valerie Aikman-Smith, Miranda Ballard,
Maxine Clark, Chloe Coker, Liz Franklin, Tori
Haschka, Vicky Jones, Jennifer Joyce, Jenny
Linford, Dan May, Jane Montgomery, Louise
Pickford, Annie Rigg, Shelagh Ryan, Belinda
Williams and Ryland Peters & Small 2016
Design and photographs © Ryland Peters
& Small 2016

ISBN: 978-1-84975-717-1

10 9 8 7 6 5 4 3 2 1

A CIP record for this book is available from the British
Library. US Library of Congress CIP data has been
applied for.

Printed and bound in China

Notes
* Recipes containing raw or partially cooked eggs
or raw fish or shellfish, should not be served to the
very young, very old, anyone with a compromised
immune system or pregnant women.
* Where a recipe calls for the grated zest of citrus
fruit, buy unwaxed fruit and wash well before using.
If you can only find treated fruit, scrub well in warm
soapy water before using.
* Ovens should be preheated to the specified
temperatures. We recommend using an oven
thermometer. If using a fan-assisted oven, adjust
temperatures according to the manufacturer's
specific instructions.

Contents

Introduction

When entertaining at home, whether you are hosting an informal supper party or planning an impressive dinner for a special occasion, you'll want your meal to get off to the best possible start.

The first course you choose to serve is all-important as it sets the stage, whets the appetite and hints at what delights are to follow. In this book, you will find a perfect selection of easy-to-prepare yet delicious recipes for small bites to serve with drinks, plated first courses and large sharing boards and platters; essentially something for every style of social occasion. Using only the freshest of produce and modern seasonings, many of the recipes have an international influence and some will be more familiar favourites.

The book features a variety of dishes taken from the sun-drenched cuisines of the Mediterranean, inspired by the exotic flavours of the Middle East, or spiced up with exciting South-east Asian and Indian ingredients. What unites all the recipes is that they are surprisingly quick and easy to prepare, full of flavour and guaranteed to impress your guests.

To take the stress out of entertaining, many of the dishes can also be made ahead of time and simply finished off as necessary once you are ready to serve. What's more, you will find that some of the recipes can be adapted to make more substantial dishes that can be enjoyed for lunch or as a light supper. In Appetizers you'll find plenty of inspiration and something to suit all tastes, enabling you to enjoy stress-free entertaining at home time and time again.

Party bites and dips

Pre-meal canapés, served as an alternative to a plated appetizer, can be a sociable and informal way of getting a dinner party started, or, if you are hosting a drinks party, the substantial bites included here will ensure that your guests don't go hungry.

Chorizo, red pepper and pea frittata bites

These bite-size frittata morsels are gorgeously colourful to look at and packed full of flavour. Delicious served either warm or at room temperature with a garlic mayonnaise on the side for dipping.

4 x 60-g/2-oz. chorizo
    sausages
16 eggs
300 ml/1¼ cups crème fraîche
a pinch each of salt and
    freshly ground black pepper
1 tablespoon olive oil
150 g/1 cup finely chopped
    red onion
1 garlic clove, crushed
130 g/1 cup fresh or frozen
    peas
1 red (bell) pepper, deseeded
    and cut into strips
60 g/1¼ cups baby spinach
    leaves
garlic mayonnaise, to serve

SERVES 8–10

Preheat the oven to 180°C (350°F) Gas 4.

Lay the chorizo sausages on a baking sheet and cook in the preheated oven for 12 minutes. Remove from the oven, drain on paper towels and cut into 1-cm/³⁄₈-inch slices. Cover and set aside.

Reduce the oven temperature to 110°C (225°F) Gas ¼.

Put the eggs in a large mixing bowl with the crème fraîche and lightly whisk to combine. Season with salt and pepper, and set aside.

Heat the oil in a large non-stick, ovenproof frying pan/skillet set over a low–medium heat. Add the onion and garlic, and sauté until soft but not coloured. Add the sliced chorizo, peas and (bell) pepper strips and cook for 2–3 minutes, stirring occasionally. Add the baby spinach and stir until the spinach just begins to wilt. Arrange the mix evenly over the base of the pan and carefully pour in the egg mixture.

Reduce the heat and gently cook the frittata, moving the egg in a little from the edge of the pan as it cooks (similar to how you would cook an omelette), using a spatula to run around the outside of the pan. You don't want to get any colour on the base of the frittata so it is important to keep the temperature low. Continue running the spatula around the pan to ensure the frittata doesn't stick.

After about 10 minutes, once it has just set on the bottom and the sides, place the pan in the oven for 15–20 minutes, until the frittata is lightly golden and just set in the middle. Remove from the oven and set aside to cool for 10 minutes. Once cool, cover the pan with a chopping board and turn it over to release the frittata. Cut it into 4-cm/1½-inch squares and transfer to a plate to serve.

Tuna empañadas

Empañadas are a popular snack in Central and South America. Serve alongside mojito cocktails at your party.

½ tablespoon olive oil

1 garlic clove, finely chopped

½ onion, diced

200g/6–7 oz. tomatoes, peeled, deseeded and diced

200 g/6½ oz. canned tuna in oil, drained and flaked

2 tablespoons tomato purée/paste

a pinch of chilli powder

½ teaspoon ground cumin

2 quantities Pastry (page 83)

salt and freshly ground black pepper, to season

vegetable oil, for frying

a 7.5-cm/3¼-inch fluted cookie cutter

MAKES 20

First prepare the filling. Heat the olive oil in a frying pan/skilletset over a medium heat. Add the garlic and onion, and fry until softened. Add the tomatoes and fry for 5 minutes, stirring often. Mix in the tuna, tomato purée/paste, chilli powder and cumin, and season with salt and pepper. Cook for 1–2 minutes.

Roll out the pastry on a lightly floured surface and cut out 20 circles using the cookie cutter. Place a teaspoon of the filling in the centre of each pastry circle, brush the edges with water and fold over, pressing together to form little parcels.

Heat vegetable oil in a large frying pan/skillet. Fry the empañadas until lightly browned on all sides. Remove from the oil using a slotted spoon, drain on paper towels and serve hot.

Smoked mackerel cherry tomatoes

These small, filled cherry tomato halves look and taste great. The salty mackerel complements the sweet, yet tangy tomato beautifully.

1 smoked mackerel fillet, skinned

1 tablespoon creamed horseradish sauce

1 tablespoon crème fraîche or sour cream

freshly ground black pepper, to season

14 cherry tomatoes

finely chopped fresh flat-leaf parsley, to garnish

MAKES 28

In a food processor, blend together the smoked mackerel, horseradish sauce and crème fraîche to form a pâté. Season with black pepper. Cover and chill for at least 30 minutes.

Next, prepare the tomatoes. Cut them in half and, using a teaspoon, carefully scoop out the soft pulp and seeds, creating 28 tomato shells.

Fill each shell with the chilled smoked mackerel pâté. Return to the fridge until you are ready to serve.

Sprinkle with finely chopped parsley and serve.

Tomato blinis

These little orange pancakes make the perfect canapé: both good-looking and tasty.

*110 g/1 scant cup plain/
all-purpose flour*
*½ teaspoon fast-action dried
yeast*
½ teaspoon white sugar
½ teaspoon salt
150 ml/⅔ cup warm whole milk
1 egg, separated
20 g/4 teaspoons butter, melted
1 tablespoon tomato purée/paste
*sour cream, Parma ham and
chopped fresh chives, to serve*

MAKES ABOUT 26

Begin by making the batter. Sift the flour into a warm mixing bowl. Stir in the yeast, sugar and salt. Whisk the warm milk into the flour mixture to form a thick batter. Whisk in the egg yolk, melted butter and tomato purée/paste. Cover and set aside in warm place to prove for 1 hour.

Preheat the oven to 110°C (225°F) Gas ¼. Whisk the egg white to stiff peaks. Gently fold the whisked egg white into the proven batter. Set a large non-stick frying pan/skillet over a medium heat. Drop spoonfuls of the batter into the pan, well spaced apart. Fry until tiny bubbles appear on the surface and the edges darken, then turn over briefly to lightly brown the other side. Transfer to a baking sheet and keep warm in the preheated oven. Cook the remaining batter in batches.

When ready to serve, top each blini with a little sour cream, a small piece of Parma ham and a sprinkling of chopped chives.

Plum tomato tartlets

Dainty, subtly flavourful tartlets make a sophisticated snack for any drinks party.

*150 g/1 cup plus 3 tablespoons
plain/all-purpose flour*
75 g/5 tablespoons butter
3 egg yolks
200 ml/scant 1 cup sour cream
*2 tablespoons chopped fresh
tarragon leaves, plus extra
to garnish*
*100 g/3 oz. soft goat's cheese,
chopped*
*12 baby plum tomatoes, halved
lengthways*
*salt and freshly ground black
pepper, to season*

a 4-cm/1½-inch cookie cutter
2 x 12-hole muffin pans, oiled

MAKES 24

First make the pastry. Blend the flour, a pinch of salt and butter in a food processor until well combined. Add 1 egg yolk and 1 tablespoon of cold water, and blend until the mixture comes together to form a ball. Wrap in clingfilm/plastic wrap and chill in the fridge for at least 30 minutes.

Preheat the oven to 200°C (400°F) Gas 6. Roll the pastry out thinly on a lightly floured surface and cut out 24 rounds using the cookie cutter. Line the muffin pans with the pastry.

To make the filling, whisk the sour cream and the remaining egg yolks together in a jug/pitcher. Season with salt and pepper and add the tarragon. Divide the goat's cheese evenly between the pastry cases, then nestle in two halved plum tomatoes in each case, skin side-down. Carefully pour in a little of the sour cream mixture, then bake in the preheated oven for 30 minutes until the filling has risen and is golden.

Garnish with tarragon if desired and serve warm.

Jalapeño poppers

Jalapeño peppers are ideal for this recipe. They have a juicy flesh that tastes delicious when combined with cheese. If they are not available, try using red Cherry Bomb chillies/chiles, which are a little sweeter and often a little hotter, too. These poppers will whet your appetite at the start of a meal.

20 jalapeño peppers
140 g/1¼ cups grated mature/
  sharp Cheddar cheese
50 g/⅓ cup plain/all-purpose
  flour
1 egg, beaten
sunflower oil, for deep-frying

a cooking thermometer
  (optional)

MAKES 20

Slit the jalapeño peppers along one side and carefully remove the seeds. Stuff the chillies/chiles generously with the grated Cheddar.

Put the flour in one shallow bowl and the beaten egg in another. Roll the jalapeño peppers in the flour, dip in the egg and then coat once more with flour, ensuring that they are completely covered.

Half-fill a large saucepan with oil. Heat until the oil reaches 190°C (375°F) on a cooking thermometer. If you don't have a cooking thermometer, the oil is ready when a 2.5-cm/1-inch cube of white bread dropped into it browns in less than 60 seconds.

Fry the jalapeño peppers in small batches for 6–7 minutes until golden. Remove with a slotted spoon and drain on paper towels before serving.

Mini corn fritters with smoked salmon and lemon cream

The three elements in this delicious trio all contribute to make these fritters decidedly tantalizing and moreish. They will disappear rapidly at a party.

225 g/2 cups grated
    courgette/zucchini
4 eggs
180 g/1⅓ cups self-raising/
    rising flour
50 g/1¾ oz. Parmesan, grated
100 ml/scant ½ cup
    buttermilk
1 teaspoon paprika
½ teaspoon cayenne pepper
1 tablespoon chopped fresh
    coriander/cilantro
fresh corn kernels cut from
    2–3 cobs
sunflower oil, for frying
salt and freshly ground black
    pepper, to season
300 g/1½ cups smoked
    salmon, to serve
chervil or chopped chives,
    to garnish

Lemon cream
250 ml/1 cup sour cream
1 tablespoon freshly squeezed
    lemon juice
1 teaspoon grated lemon zest
¼ teaspoon sea salt

MAKES 30–35

Put the grated courgette/zucchini into a colander set over a large mixing bowl. Sprinkle with ½ teaspoon of salt and leave for 30 minutes–1 hour so they release their moisture. Squeeze the grated courgette/zucchini with your hands to get rid of as much moisture as possible and set aside.

In a large, clean, dry mixing bowl, lightly whisk the eggs.

Add the flour, grated Parmesan, buttermilk, paprika, cayenne pepper, ½ teaspoon of salt, black pepper and chopped coriander/cilantro.

Stir in the squeezed courgette/zucchini and corn kernels, ensuring the vegetables are evenly coated in batter.

Add enough sunflower oil to thinly cover the bottom of a non-stick frying pan/skillet. Drop small spoonfuls of batter into the pan using a teaspoon and cook for about 2 minutes on each side, until golden brown. Drain on paper towels, then transfer to a clean baking sheet. Cook the remaining batter in the same way, adding a little more oil to the pan each time, if required. If you are not going to assemble the blinis straight away, cool completely, cover with clingfilm/plastic wrap and set aside.

To make the lemon cream, combine the sour cream, lemon juice and zest and salt in a small bowl. Add the salt and stir through.

Arrange the blinis on a serving platter, top with a ribbon of smoked salmon and a dollop of lemon cream. Garnish with chervil or chopped chives and a sprinkle of freshly ground black pepper.

Cherry tomato and basil bruschetta

Juicy tomatoes contrast nicely with the crunchiness of the baked bread in this vibrant, classic Italian snack. Serve as a rustic start to an evening meal or as a summertime canapé.

1 slender baguette/French stick

2 teaspoons good-quality olive oil

12 red and yellow cherry tomatoes, quartered

1 teaspoon balsamic vinegar

a pinch of salt

1 garlic clove

4–6 fresh basil leaves, plus extra to garnish

freshly ground black pepper, to serve

MAKES ABOUT 12

Preheat the oven to 200°C (400°F) Gas 6.

Slice the baguette into 1-cm/^{3}/$_8$-inch thick slices. Transfer to a baking sheet and lightly brush each slice with half of the oil. Bake in the preheated oven for 20 minutes, until pale gold and crisp. Remove from the oven and set aside to cool.

Meanwhile, mix together the cherry tomatoes with the remaining olive oil, balsamic vinegar, salt and whole garlic clove in a large bowl. Shred the basil leaves and mix in. Set aside to allow the flavours to infuse while the baguette slices bake and cool.

Discard the garlic clove from the tomato mixture, then spoon onto each slice of bread. Garnish with basil leaves and sprinkle with black pepper. Serve at once.

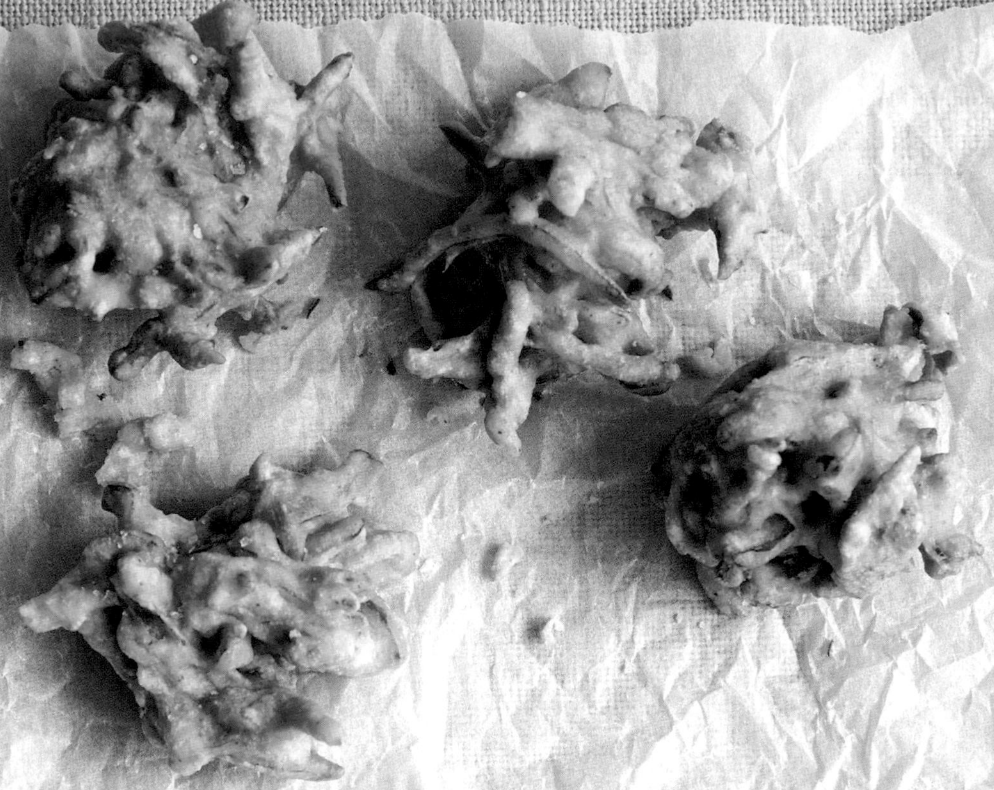

Shallot and banana bhajis

These crunchy morsels are best served as soon as they come out of the pan and make a good snack alongside a bowl of sweet and sour tamarind or coriander/cilantro chutney as a dip. Try other ingredients such as spinach or grated carrot.

175 g/a scant 1½ cups
    chickpea/gram flour, sifted
2 shallots, finely chopped
1 potato (about 100 g/3½ oz.),
    peeled and grated
1 teaspoon grated fresh ginger
1 teaspoon finely chopped
    fresh green chilli/chile
½ teaspoon chilli powder
½ unripe banana, chopped
¾ teaspoon salt
vegetable oil, for frying

MAKES ABOUT 20

Mix all of the ingredients apart from the oil in a bowl and add just enough water (about 200 ml/generous ¾ cup) to make a mixture that holds together and can be dropped off a spoon.

In a medium saucepan, heat enough oil to deep-fry about 6 small bhajis at a time. The oil should be hot enough to brown a cube of bread in 30 seconds (around 180–190°C/360–375°F).

When it is hot enough, use a pair of spoons to drop walnut-sized balls of the mixture into the oil. Cook the bhajis until golden brown, turning over as they cook, then remove with a slotted spoon and drain on paper towels. Cook the rest of the bhajis in the same way in batches.

The bhajis are best served straight away, but can be cooked in advance and reheated if more convenient.

Black lentil pancakes with mint raita

Black beluga lentils are best for these little pancakes, as they hold their shape well when cooked. Puy lentils could also be used as an alternative.

125 g/⅔ cup dried black beluga lentils
75 g/⅔ cup plain/all-purpose flour
1 egg
150 ml/⅔ cup whole milk
1 teaspoon ground cumin
½–1 teaspoon salt
1–2 dried red chillies/chiles, deseeded and chopped
2 tablespoons chopped coriander/cilantro
300 ml/1¼ cups plain yogurt
6-cm/2½-inch piece of cucumber
2 tablespoons chopped fresh mint, plus leaves to garnish
¼ teaspoon ground cumin
vegetable oil, for frying

MAKES ABOUT 20

Rinse and drain the lentils, then put in a large saucepan with water to cover them. Cover the pan and bring to the boil. Turn down the heat and simmer for 25–30 minutes until tender. Drain and set aside.

Whisk together the flour, egg, milk, cumin and salt until smooth. Stir in the lentils, the chillies/chiles and the coriander/cilantro and set aside.

Make the raita by beating the yogurt until smooth, then stir in the peeled and grated cucumber, chopped mint and cumin.

Heat a tablespoon of oil in a large frying pan/skillet or pancake pan. Drop spoonfuls of the batter into the hot pan/skillet, smoothing out the surface of each as you go. You should be able to make 6–7 at a time. Cook for approximately 5 minutes, until the undersides are beginning to brown, then turn over with a spatula and cook the other side. Continue until all of the batter is used.

Serve warm with a teaspoonful of mint raita on each pancake and a mint leaf to garnish.

Devils on horseback

There's a debate about when these bites had their 'heyday', which only means they've never gone away. To make the luxurious variation Angels on Horseback, use smoked oysters in place of the prunes or dates.

6 slices prosciutto
12 whole blanched almonds
12 stoned/pitted dried dates
  or prunes

MAKES 12

Cut each slice of prosciutto lengthways down the middle (kitchen scissors work best for this) to make 12 half-slices.

For each 'devil', put an almond in the middle of a pitted date, wrap a half-slice of prosciutto tightly around the fruit and then lay it on a baking sheet. Repeat to make 12 'devils' in total.

Preheat the grill/broiler to high.

Grill/broil the 'devils' for about 5 minutes, until the prosciutto starts to brown and crisp. Turn the 'devils' over and grill/broil for a further 2–3 minutes. Push a toothpick through the middle of each one and serve immediately.

Horses on devilback

The tables are turned – fair's fair –and it is now the horse's turn. Here, slices of chutney-filled ham are threaded through the prunes before grilling/broiling. A smear of mango chutney on the ham adds balancing sweetness.

12 stoned/pitted dried prunes
12 slices saucisson sec or
   6 slices Serrano ham
6 teaspoons mango chutney

MAKES 12

Make sure that the pitted prunes each have a hole that goes all the way throught the middle. If you are using Serrano ham, cut each slice lengthways down the middle (kitchen scissors work best for this) to make 12 half-slices.

For each 'horse', take a slice of saucisson sec or half-slice of Serrano ham. Spread ½ teaspoon mango chutney over each slice then roll the meat into a tight tube, and thread it through the middle of a prune. Lay it on a baking sheet and repeat to make 12 'horses' in total.

Preheat the grill/broiler to high.

Grill/broil the 'horses' for about 2 minutes, to warm through, turning once. Push a toothpick through the middle of each one and serve immediately.

Chorizo and scallop skewers

This is as lovely a combination of textures as it is of flavours. The scallops become slightly pink from the chorizo oil, and the taste of paprika permeates the soft flesh. This dish is a great store-cupboard standby: frozen scallops cook beautifully, and chorizo has such a long shelf-life that you'll never be caught short in the event of an impromtu tapas party.

12 shelled scallops (or frozen scallops, defrosted)

12 x 1 om/¾-inch cubes of chorizo

salt and freshly ground black or pink pepper, to season

olive oil, for frying

paprika, for sprinkling (optional)

MAKES 12

First fry the scallops in a little olive oil in a frying pan/skillet over a high heat for 1 minute on each side, until cooked. Add a good twist of black or pink pepper, then add the chorizo cubes and fry for a further 2–3 minutes, turning and stirring everything often.

Remove the chorizo and scallops from the pan and leave until cool enough to handle, then thread one scallop and chorizo cube onto a toothpick. Thread the scallop on first as the chorizo does a better job of gripping the stick.

Repeat to make 12 canapés in total. Serve immediately, while still warm, sprinkled with a little paprika, if you like.

Variation: You can always add a little chilli powder or paprika to coat the scallops before cooking, but enough flavourful oil will come out of good-quality chorizo as you fry it.

Chicken tikka bites

The lime leaves give a delightful floral fragrance to this dish and a hot Madras relish livens things up.

450 g/1 lb. chicken fillets
a handful of lime leaves
a 5-cm/2-inch piece of fresh ginger,
    peeled and chopped
3 garlic cloves, roughly chopped
60 ml/¼ cup vegetable oil
grated zest and juice of 2 limes
1 tablespoon curry powder
1 teaspoon chilli powder
½ teaspoon smoked paprika
10 g/½ cup coriander/cilantro

MAKES 12 SKEWERS

Mango Madras relish
flesh of 1 ripe mango
1 fresh red chilli/chile, finely diced
grated zest and juice of 1 lime
1 tablespoon grated fresh ginger
2 spring onions/scallions, sliced
1 garlic clove, finely chopped
½ teaspoon Madras curry powder
¼ teaspoon smoked paprika
60 ml/¼ cup rice wine vinegar
1 tablespoon sesame oil
2 tablespoons peanut oil
salt, to season

First make the relish. Cut the mango flesh into 5-mm/½-inch cubes and put in a bowl. Add the chilli/chile, lime zest and juice, ginger, onions, garlic, curry powder and paprika. Toss to combine. In a small bowl, whisk together the vinegar, sesame and peanut oils. Pour over the mango mix and stir well to coat. Season with salt and chill in the fridge until ready to serve.

Cut the chicken fillets into 3.5-cm/1½-inch chunks. Thread a piece of chicken onto one of soaked wooden skewers, then a lime leaf, and another piece of chicken. Repeat until you have used up all of the chicken and the lime leaves. Put the skewers in a large shallow bowl and set aside. Put the chopped ginger and garlic, coconut oil, lime zest and juice, curry powder, chilli powder, paprika and coriander/cilantro in a food processor. Blend until smooth. Pour the sauce over the chicken skewers, coating the meat. Cover and refrigerate for 2–4 hours.

Preheat the grill/broiler to medium. Lay the skewers directly in the grill pan and cook for 4 minutes on each side, until the chicken is cooked through. Serve with the mango Madras relish.

Greek fava dip

One of the most popular appetizers in Greek tavernas is fava, a tasty dip made from tiny yellow split peas (not broad/fava beans). The peas grown on Santorini are most prized, but they also grow wild in other parts of the Mediterranean.

50 ml/3 tablespoons olive oil
1 onion, finely diced
250 g/8 oz. Greek broad/fava peas, skinned and split
2 fresh or dried bay leaves
1 teaspoon dried oregano
salt and freshly ground black pepper, to season
freshly squeezed lemon juice, to taste

To serve
1 tablespoon pickled caper berries, drained
1 sweet red onion, very thinly sliced, or grilled artichoke hearts, cut in half
toasted pitta bread or breadsticks

SERVES 6

Heat half of the olive oil in a saucepan and add the diced onion to soften. Add 500 ml/2 cups of water, bring to the boil and stir in the split peas. Add the bay leaves and the oregano and simmer, covered, for 1–2 hours, or until the water has been absorbed and the fava has become completely mushy. Stir from time to time to prevent it sticking to the bottom of the pan and add more hot water if necessary.

When it is cooked, allow to cool slightly, remove the bay leaves, then blitz to a purée in a food processor. Stir in the rest of the olive oil, then season with salt, pepper and lemon juice to taste. Dilute with a little cold water to get the right consistency.

Serve cold in a shallow bowl, with the caper berries and onion slices or artichokes and toasted pitta bread or breadsticks to dip into the communal bowl.

Lebanese houmous

There must be thousands of recipes for houmous, but this method – not the quickest, but arguably the best – is how Mohammed Alden, owner and chef of Al Waha, the popular Lebanese restaurant in Notting Hill, London, makes it.

200 g/1¼ cups dried chickpeas, soaked overnight and drained
½ teaspoon bicarbonate of/baking soda
60 ml/¼ cup very cold freshly squeezed lemon juice
60 g/¼ cup tahini (about 3 tablespoons)
salt, to season
olive oil, paprika, chopped fresh flat-leaf parsley and hot pitta breads, to serve

SERVES 4–6

Put the chickpeas in a large saucepan with double the amount of fresh water. Add the bicarbonate of/baking soda and bring to the boil, cover, then simmer until the chickpeas are cooked – about 1–1½ hours.

Take the saucepan off the heat and put under cold running water. This will shock the skins into cracking, so that they come off easily and float to the surface. Gently stir the chickpeas, and as the skins surface, remove them with a slotted spoon. Continue until most of the skins have been removed.

Strain the water from the chickpeas and leave in a colander in the fridge, preferably overnight, to drain thoroughly. Squeeze the lemon juice and chill in the fridge overnight, or add ice cubes for a quick chill.

Put the chickpeas into a food processor and blitz until you have a smooth paste, then add the tahini and process again. The mixture should be very smooth but still a little firm. Add the lemon juice and blend again, then add salt to taste.

Finally, leave the mixture for 15–20 minutes to allow the flavour to develop. If it is too thick, dilute with more lemon juice and crushed ice.

Put the mixture in a dish, then make swirly grooves in the surface with the back of a spoon and drizzle with some olive oil. Sprinkle with paprika and chopped parsley, and serve with hot pitta bread.

It will keep perfectly well in the fridge, covered with clingfilm/plastic wrap, for several days.

Roasted aubergine/eggplant and red onion dip with paprika pitta crisps

This rich and earthy dip is very similar to the popular Middle Eastern dish baba ganoush. It can be made the day before, and is easily adapted to include other spices such as cumin, fennel or chilli/chile. You can also bake the pittas in cayenne pepper, sumac or five-spice powder for a slightly different flavour.

1 large aubergine/eggplant
2 red onions, quartered
4 garlic cloves, unpeeled
grated zest and freshly
   squeezed juice of 1 lemon
a pinch of sugar
4 tablespoons/¼ cup olive oil
salt and freshly ground black
   pepper, to season

Paprika pitta crisps
   (optional)
5 pitta breads, halved
   lengthways and cut into
   strips
1 tablespoon paprika (plain
   or smoked)
2 tablespoons olive oil

To serve
2 tablespoons pomegranate
   seeds (optional)
1 tablespoon extra virgin olive
   oil, for drizzling

SERVES 4–6

To make the roasted aubergine/eggplant and red onion dip, preheat the oven to 190°C (375°F) Gas 5.

Put the aubergine/eggplant, onions and garlic on a baking sheet, then in the preheated oven. Bake for 40–45 minutes until soft, but remove the garlic after 10–15 minutes and the onions after 20–25 minutes.

When cooked, cut the aubergine/eggplant in half, scoop out the flesh, and put it in a blender. Squeeze the garlic cloves out of their skins, remove and discard the soft cores and skins of the onions.

Blend the aubergine/eggplant, onions, garlic, lemon zest, sugar, olive oil, and a pinch of salt and pepper to a purée. Taste and adjust the seasoning with lemon juice, sugar, salt and pepper, if needed.

To make the paprika pitta crisps, turn the oven up to 200°C (400°F) Gas 6. Drizzle a clean baking sheet with the olive oil, then sprinkle with the paprika and a pinch of salt and pepper. Put the pitta bread strips on the baking sheet and mix to coat. Bake in the oven for 8 minutes until slightly coloured and crisp.

Spoon the dip into a serving bowl and sprinkle with pomegranate seeds, if using. Drizzle with extra virgin olive oil and serve with the pitta crisps on the side for dipping.

Sweet potato houmous with breadsticks

This velvety smooth sweet potato houmous dip makes an interesting change from the more familiar plain chickpea version. The breadsticks are simple to make and their crunchy texture makes them the perfect accompaniment here.

1 sweet potato, unpeeled
3 garlic cloves, unpeeled
200 g/7 oz. canned chickpeas
1 fresh red chilli/chile, very finely chopped
a handful of fresh coriander/cilantro leaves, chopped
2 tablespoons olive oil
grated zest and freshly squeezed juice of ½ lime
salt and freshly ground black pepper, to season

Breadsticks (optional)
300 g/2¼ cups plain/all-purpose flour
2 teaspoons fast-action dried yeast
2 teaspoons salt
1 teaspoon sugar
4 tablespoons/¼ cup olive oil
120–150 ml/½–⅔ cup lukewarm water
a pinch of mixed dried herbs
a pinch of cayenne pepper

SERVES 4–6

To make the sweet potato houmous, preheat the oven to 180°C (350°F) Gas 4.

Put the sweet potato in a roasting pan and cook in the preheated oven for 30–40 minutes until very soft. Add the garlic cloves about 20 minutes before the end of the cooking time.

Remove from the oven and, when cool enough to handle, remove and discard the skins from the sweet potato and garlic cloves. Put the chickpeas, chilli/chile, coriander/cilantro, olive oil and lime zest in a food processor and blitz until they reach the desired consistency. Season with salt, pepper and lime juice to taste.

To make the breadsticks, reduce the heat of the oven to 170°C (340°F) Gas 4.

Combine the flour, yeast, salt and sugar in a bowl. Make a well in the centre, pour in the olive oil and water, and stir until well combined and the dough comes together. It should be soft but not sticky.

Knead the dough for about 10 minutes by hand, cover with oiled clingfilm/plastic wrap or a damp cloth and leave to rise in a warm place for 40 minutes–1 hour, or until doubled in size.

Divide the dough in half and keep half wrapped up so that it does not dry out. Roll half the dough out into a flat rectangle about 0.5–1-cm/¼–⅜-inch thick, then cut it into 1-cm/⅜-inch-wide strips. Roll the strips into pencil-width tubes. Repeat with the other half of the dough. Spread the mixed dried herbs, cayenne pepper and a pinch each of salt and pepper on a board, then roll the breadsticks in them. Arrange on a floured baking sheet and bake in the preheated oven for 20–30 minutes until golden. Cool on a wire rack.

When ready to serve, spoon the sweet potato houmous into a serving bowl and serve with the cooled breadsticks on the side for dipping.

Bacon bites

These are lovely little crackers to serve as canapés. You can vary the ingredients: chives work well, as does a nice strong Gruyère. Add a few chilli/hot red pepper flakes and, if you have a jar open, some finely chopped sun-dried tomatoes.

40 g/1½ oz. very thinly sliced pancetta or Parma ham

50 g/3½ tablespoons butter, softened

150 g/1 cup plus 2½ tablespoons plain/all-purpose flour

a pinch of salt

50 g/⅔ cup finely grated Parmesan cheese

1 teaspoon very finely chopped fresh rosemary needles

1 egg

a cookie cutter (optional)

a baking sheet lined with baking parchment

MAKES ABOUT 20

Preheat the oven to 180°C (350°F) Gas 4.

Lay the pancetta out on a non-stick baking sheet and cook for 5 minutes, or until crisp, taking care not to let it burn. Remove from the oven, cool slightly, chop into pieces and set aside.

Rub the butter, flour and salt together in a large mixing bowl until the mixture resembles fine breadcrumbs. Stir in the Parmesan and rosemary. Add the egg and chopped pancetta and bring everything together to form a soft dough.

Roll the dough out between two sheets of baking parchment to a thickness of roughly 2.5 mm/$\frac{1}{16}$ inch and cut into squares or cut out shapes using a cookie cutter. Arrange on the prepared baking sheet and bake in the preheated oven for 8–10 minutes, until golden and firm.

Store in an airtight container and eat within 3 days.

Curry cashew crunch cookies

These crunchy little treats have a hint of curry, a touch of cumin and are speckled with curry-flavoured cashews; a great little savoury combo that's perfect to offer round with pre-dinner drinks.

150 g/1 cup plus
 2½ tablespoons plain/
 all-purpose flour
½ teaspoon salt
1 tablespoon mild curry
 powder
1 generous teaspoon cumin
 seeds
75 g/5 tablespoons butter
1 egg, beaten
50 g/1½ oz. curry-flavoured
 cashew nuts, roughly
 chopped

2 baking sheets lined with
 baking parchment

MAKES ABOUT 20

Preheat the oven to 180°C (350°F) Gas 4.

Put the flour, salt and curry powder into a large mixing bowl. Stir in the cumin seeds. Rub the butter into the mixture until it resembles fine breadcrumbs, then add the beaten egg. Draw everything together to form a smooth dough.

Knead the cashew nuts into the dough. Roll into a log shape and wrap tightly in clingfilm/plastic wrap. Refrigerate for 30 minutes or so to firm up.

Unwrap the dough and cut into slices just under 1-cm/³⁄₈-inch thick. Arrange on the prepared baking sheets, leaving a little space for spreading between each one. Bake in the preheated oven for about 10 minutes, until crisp and golden.

Leave to cool for 5 minutes or so, before transferring to a wire rack to cool completely. Store in an airtight container and eat within 5 days.

Soups and salads

Fresh, lightly flavoured soups make the perfect
start to any meal, and chilled soups are a sophisticated
choice for summer eating. Salads make the best of
seasonal produce and often take little or no advance
preparation, leaving the busy host free to focus
on the main event.

Green tomato and sorrel soup

Tangy green tomatoes and lemon-flavoured sorrel combine to make a deliciously refreshing and sophisticated-tasting cold soup. If you can't source fresh sorrel, leaf spinach with a squeeze of lemon juice makes a tasty alternative. Serve as an appetizer with good sourdough bread and butter on the side.

50 g/2 cups sorrel leaves
25 g/2 tablespoons butter
1 shallot, finely chopped
500 g/1 lb. green tomatoes, roughly chopped
600 ml/2½ cups chicken or vegetable stock
salt and freshly ground black pepper, to season
4 tablespoon plain yogurt, to garnish

SERVES 4

First, prepare the sorrel. Tear the leaves off the tough ribs and shred the leaves finely.

Melt the butter in a heavy-bottomed saucepan or pot set over a medium heat. Add the shallot and fry gently for 2–3 minutes until softened, stirring now and then. Add the tomatoes and shredded sorrel leaves and continue to cook, stirring often, for 2–3 minutes.

Add the stock to the pan, stir to combine and season with salt and pepper. Bring to the boil, reduce the heat, cover and simmer gently for 25 minutes.

Blend the soup until smooth, then strain through a fine mesh sieve/strainer set over a jug/pitcher. Cool completely, then chill in the fridge for at least 2 hours.

Serve each portion garnished with a swirl of plain yogurt and seasoned with a crack of black pepper.

Lobster bisque

This bisque is the epitome of indulgence – lobster with cream and brandy. Not an everyday dish, but every cook should have a recipe for very special occasions. You can replace one of the lobsters with crab meat, adding it just before serving.

2 large cooked lobsters

150 g/1¼ sticks butter

2 onions, diced

4 small potatoes, peeled and diced

1 fennel bulb, sliced

4 celery sticks, sliced

1 large leek (white only), sliced

4 garlic cloves, crushed

a good pinch of ground ginger (optional)

2 bay leaves

2 sprigs of fresh tarragon or 1 generous teaspoon dried

2 litres/quarts fish stock

200 g/7 oz. fresh or canned chopped tomatoes

200 ml/¾ cup white wine

4 tablespoons tomato purée/ paste

150 ml/⅔ cup vermouth plus 150 ml/⅔ cup Cognac, or 300 ml/1¼ cups of either

a good pinch of cayenne pepper

a dash of Tabasco (optional)

250 ml/1 cup double/heavy cream, plus a little extra to garnish

freshly squeezed lemon juice, to season

salt and ground black pepper

freshly snipped chives, to garnish

SERVES 6

Remove all the meat from the cooked lobster tails and claws, and set aside. Reserve the shells to flavour the soup.

Melt the butter in a large saucepan and add all the vegetables, garlic, ground ginger, if using, and herbs, then add the lobster shells. Pour in the stock, tomatoes and white wine, cover and simmer gently for about 1 hour.

Some people liquidize the shell and all, but if you worry about the sharpness of the blade on your stick blender, remove the shells from the pan, and blend all the other bits until smooth. If brave, and you have strong blades, you can whizz the lot! Pass the soup through a fine mesh sieve/strainer twice, using a ladle to force the purée through to achieve a fine, smooth base. Pour the soup into a clean pan and stir in the tomato purée/paste.

Put the vermouth and Cognac in a separate small pan and set over a high heat. Very carefully flambé the liquid by using a long kitchen match to set the alcohol alight. Simply touch a lit match to the very edge of the pan and the alcohol fumes will catch – stand well back! The flames will die down once all the alcohol has burned away. When this has happened, pour the remaining liquid into the soup.

Add the cayenne pepper and a little splash of Tabasco, if you like it hot. Stir in the cream and a squeeze of lemon juice to lift the flavour. If it is a tiny bit bitter, add a little sugar to balance the flavours. Season with salt and black pepper. Lastly, and just before you want to eat it, gently warm the soup to a simmer and add the reserved lobster meat to heat through.

Serve in elegant bowls, garnished with a swirl of cream and sprinkled with snipped chives.

Fennel and courgette/ zucchini soup with crème fraîche and Parmesan

This tasty soup is an attempt to recreate the deliciousness of fennel gratin in soup form. Fresh courgettes/zucchini make a summery seasonal addition, while the rocket/arugula gives the soup a lovely peppery hit and the crème fraîche, although rich, lifts the flavour for a slightly fresher note.

75 g/5 tablespoons butter

1 large onion, diced

2 potatoes, peeled and diced

2 small fennel bulbs, thinly sliced

2 garlic cloves, crushed

1.75 litres/7⅓ cups vegetable stock

2 courgettes/zucchini, diced

a large handful of rocket/ arugula leaves

100 ml/7 tablespoons double/heavy cream

200 ml/¾ cup crème fraîche

2 tablespoons freshly grated Parmesan cheese, plus extra to garnish

salt and ground black pepper, to season

a small bunch of fresh flat-leaf parsley, roughly chopped, to garnish

SERVES 6

Melt the butter in a large saucepan and add the onion, potatoes, fennel and garlic. Cook for a few minutes over a medium heat to soften, then pour over the stock. Bring the liquid to a simmer and cook for about 15 minutes, until the fennel is tender.

Add the courgettes/zucchini and rocket/arugula leaves, and cook for a further 4 minutes. Take the pan off the heat and blend with a handheld electric blender until very smooth. Stir in the cream and crème fraîche and the grated Parmesan, and season well with salt and black pepper.

Ladle the soup into bowls and serve garnished with lots of freshly chopped parsley and a sprinkling of Parmesan on top.

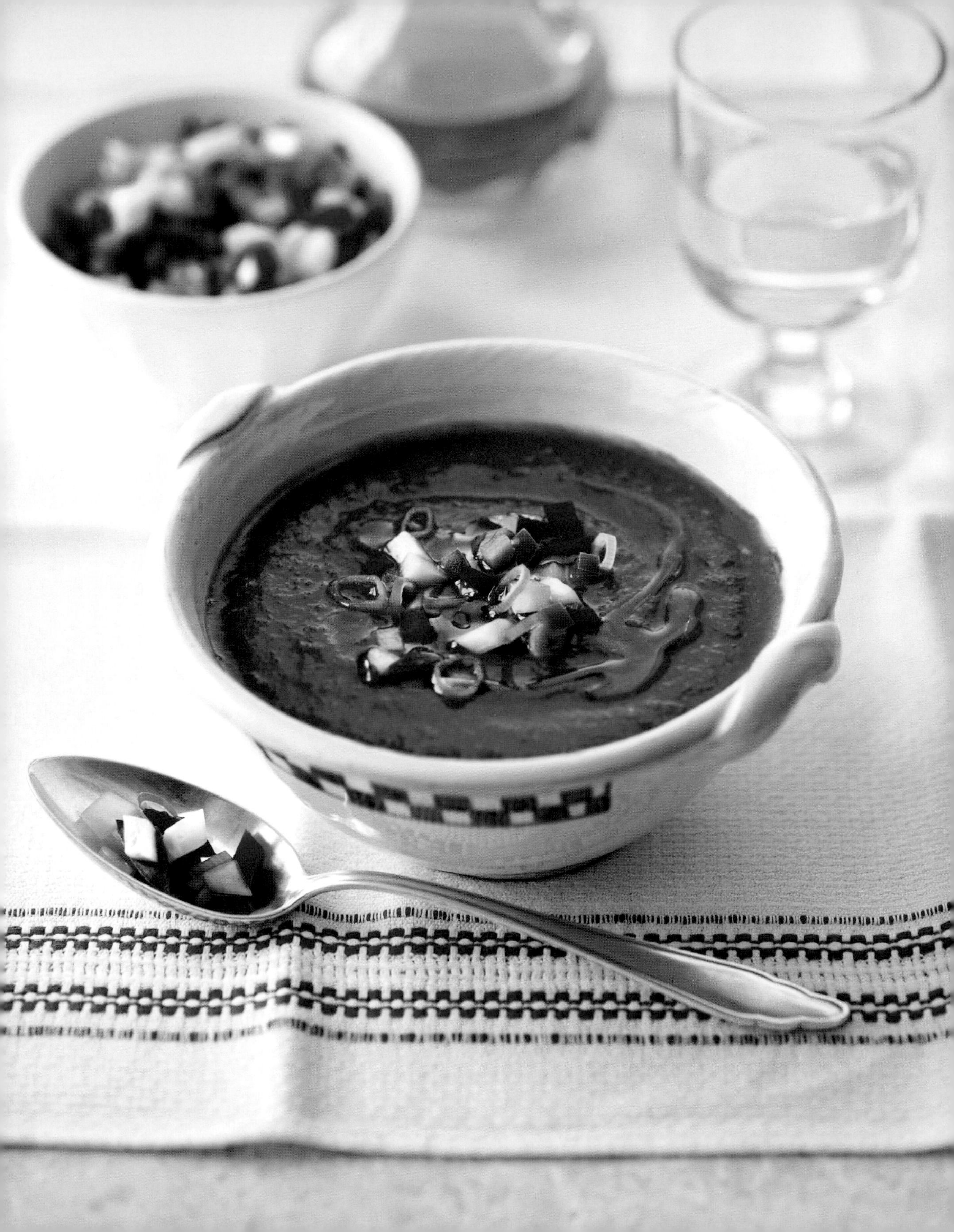

Majorcan gazpacho

Gazpacho is a brilliant Spanish chilled soup. Best served as cold as possible, it is the perfect appetizer to have before a barbecue on a summer's day or serve in small shot glasses as a canapé or part of a tapas spread.

12 very ripe tomatoes, peeled (see Tip), deseeded and roughly diced

¾ cucumber, peeled and deseeded

2 red (bell) peppers, deseeded and diced

4 spring onions/scallions, (whites only), sliced

1 red and 1 green chilli/chile, deseeded and diced

3 garlic cloves, crushed

600 ml/2½ cups thick tomato juice

1 tablespoon tomato purée/paste

1 slice of white bread, crusts removed, soaked in 1 tablespoon tarragon or white wine vinegar

150 ml/⅔ cup extra virgin olive oil, plus extra to drizzle

a pinch of celery salt

a dash of Tabasco

freshly ground black pepper, to season

To serve
finely diced red and green (bell) peppers, cucumber, tomato and spring onion/scallion greens

sweet balsamic glaze

SERVES 6

Put all the vegetables, chillies/chiles, garlic, tomato juice, tomato purée/paste and soaked bread in the bowl of a blender and whizz until smooth(ish). You may need to do this in batches depending on the size of your blender. Alternatively, you can put them in a large saucepan and blend using a handheld electric blender. Gradually trickle in the olive oil while blending – this will give a gloss and richness to the soup, and balance the acidity. Once all the oil has been incorporated, season with celery salt, Tabasco and ground black pepper. Put in the fridge to chill.

Combine all the finely diced vegetables for the garnish in a small mixing bowl.

Once well chilled, ladle the soup into bowls and serve garnished with a spoonful of the diced vegetables, with any extra served in a bowl on the side. Drizzle over a little sweet balsamic glaze and extra virgin olive oil, to serve.

Tip: For an easy way to peel tomatoes, bring a pan of salted water to a simmer. With a sharp knife, cut a cross in the base of each tomato and put in the pan of hot water. Leave for 30–40 seconds (the time may vary depending on the ripeness of the tomato), then transfer to a bowl of cold water. The skin should now easily peel away at the point of the cross cut.

Chilled cucumber yogurt soup with red chilli/chile and mint salsa

This soup is deliciously light and refreshing, with a spicy kick from the salsa. Why not serve in small portions in place of a more traditional sorbet course?

15 g/1 tablespoon butter
4 shallots, diced
2 cucumbers, peeled and
    deseeded
a small bunch of fresh dill,
    chopped
leaves from a few sprigs of fresh
    mint, chopped
a small bunch of fresh chives,
    chopped
1 slice white bread
3 tomatoes, peeled (see Tip,
    page 49), deseeded and
    diced
400 g/1²/₃ cups thick Greek
    yogurt
200 ml/³/₄ cup double/heavy
    cream
1 litre/4 cups vegetable stock
½ teaspoon cumin seeds
½ teaspoon caraway seeds
grated zest of 1 lemon
2 teaspoons Dijon mustard
salt and ground black pepper,
    to season

Salsa
2 red chillies/chiles, finely
    diced
freshly squeezed lemon juice,
    to taste
a drizzle of olive oil

SERVES 6–8

In a small frying pan/skillet, melt the butter and sauté the shallots for a few minutes, until softened, then leave to cool.

Cut a small chunk from one of the cucumbers and set aside to use in the salsa, along with a little of each of the chopped herbs.

Put the shallots and all the other soup ingredients in a blender and whizz until smooth – the soup should be the consistency of double/heavy cream. The herbs need to be a balance of all three – although the mint will be fairly dominant in the overall freshness and flavour of the soup – so taste and add more of any herb that may be lacking. Season to taste with salt and black pepper, then put the soup in the fridge to chill for at least 1 hour before serving.

To make the salsa, finely dice the reserved cucumber. Combine it with the red chilli/chile and reserved herbs. Mix with a little lemon juice and a drizzle of olive oil to bind, then chill until needed.

Serve the soup in small chilled glasses with a teaspoon and garnish with the pretty salsa.

Cream of celeriac/celery root and white bean soup with toasted hazelnuts and truffle oil

When you taste a visually honest soup such as this, it can be a challenge to identify all the different flavours coming through. Good old ugly celeriac/celery root has such a wonderful nutty sweetness, while the starch from the smooth white beans gives the soup richness, and the hazelnuts and truffle oil work to bring both texture and forest-floor flavours.

150 g/1 cup hazelnuts

90 ml/6 tablespoons olive oil

8 banana shallots, finely diced

2 garlic cloves, roughly chopped

2 celeriac/celery root, peeled and diced

2 celery sticks, sliced

2 bay leaves

2 litres/quarts chicken stock

a 400-g/14-oz. can cannellini beans, drained

180 ml/^{3}/$_4$ cup double/heavy cream

freshly squeezed lemon juice, to taste

salt and ground black pepper, to season

truffle oil, for drizzling

SERVES 6–8

To toast the hazelnuts, put them in a roasting pan and pop them in a medium–hot oven for about 10 minutes, until they are just golden and smelling lovely. Tip the toasted nuts into a kitchen cloth and rub well to remove the skins, then roughly chop.

Put the olive oil, shallots, garlic, celeriac/celery root, celery and bay leaves in a saucepan and toss over medium–high heat for a few minutes, until beginning to soften. Add the stock to the pan along with the cannellini beans and three-quarters of the toasted hazelnuts. Cover the pan and simmer gently for about 15–20 minutes, until the celeriac/celery root is very tender. Take the pan off the heat and remove the bay leaves.

With a handheld electric blender, whizz the soup until very smooth, then stir in the cream and blend briefly again until well mixed. If you think the soup is a little thin, allow to simmer gently over very low heat to reduce down – this should be a smooth, velvety soup. When you are happy with the consistency, season with salt and pepper and lift the flavour with a squeeze of lemon juice.

Ladle the soup into bowls, scatter the reserved chopped hazelnuts over the top and drizzle with truffle oil to serve.

Chilled smoked salmon, avocado and chive soup

This is a lovely way to enjoy avocado in the summer and is a real treat when served with hot, crusty garlic bread. Avocado, salmon and chives are a marriage made in heaven and really worth a try.

5 spring onions/scallions
5 ripe avocados, peeled,
    stoned/pitted and diced
2 garlic cloves, crushed
2 green chillies/chiles, sliced
½ cucumber, peeled, deseeded
    and diced
60 g/¼ cup cream cheese
60 g/¼ cup sour cream
1 litre/4 cups vegetable or
    chicken stock
5 slices of smoked salmon, cut
    into fine ribbons and any
    brown meat removed
a small bunch of fresh chives,
    finely snipped
freshly squeezed lime juice,
    to taste
salt and ground black pepper,
    to season

Salsa
a small bunch of fresh
    coriander/cilantro, chopped
grated zest and freshly
    squeezed juice of 1 lime
2 tablespoons olive oil
4 ripe tomatoes, peeled (see
    Tip, page 49), deseeded
    and finely diced
½ red onion, finely diced
¼ cucumber, finely diced

SERVES 6–8

Trim the greens from the spring onions/scallions and set them aside to use in the salsa. Roughly chop the spring onion/scallion whites and put them in the bowl of a food processor along with the avocado, garlic, chillies/chiles, cucumber, cream cheese, sour cream and about one-quarter of the stock to loosen. Blitz on full speed until smooth, then pour into a large bowl and stir in the remaining stock slowly, to achieve a good even consistency – it should not be too thin, but should coat the back of a spoon. Avocados vary and the soup's consistency will depend on their fatty or more watery nature, so you may not need to add all of the stock.

Season the soup with salt and pepper and add the smoked salmon (reserve a few ribbons to garnish), the finely snipped chives and a good squeeze of fresh lime juice to balance the acidity and richness. Cover the soup and chill.

To make the salsa, finely chop the reserved spring onion/scallion greens, put them in a mixing bowl with the other salsa ingredients and mix gently.

Serve a generous amount of avocado soup with a lovely spoonful of salsa piled in the centre, and a few of the reserved salmon ribbons to garnish.

Butternut squash and coconut milk soup

This soup is warming and supremely satisfying. Not only does it taste fantastic, combining hints of the East with all the best bits of a cool, crisp day, but the colour is superb. Why not make it a staple part of your winter menu, and keep a huge pan of it on the go for get-togethers during the colder months.

1 butternut squash, peeled, deseeded and cut into 2-cm/1-inch cubes
1 sweet potato, peeled and cut into 2-cm/1-inch cubes
3 garlic cloves, unpeeled and bruised
4 tablespoons olive oil
1 onion, finely chopped
1 celery stick, finely chopped
2 teaspoons vegetable stock/ bouillon powder
1 medium–hot red chilli/chile, deseeded and finely chopped
a 2.5-cm/1-inch piece of fresh ginger, peeled and grated
a 400-ml/14-oz. can of coconut milk
salt and freshly ground black pepper, to season
chopped fresh coriander/ cilantro, to garnish
toasted sesame oil, to drizzle

SERVES 4–6

Preheat the oven to 180°C (350°F) Gas 4.

Put the butternut squash, sweet potato and garlic into a roasting dish, drizzle half of the olive oil over the top, cover loosely with foil and roast in the preheated oven for about 40 minutes, or until the squash, potato and garlic are soft.

Meanwhile, heat the remaining olive oil in a saucepan over a low heat and gently fry the onion and celery for about 10 minutes, or until soft. Add the stock/bouillon powder, chilli/chile and ginger – it will help if you add a couple of tablespoons of water at this point to stop the stock/bouillon from sticking to the bottom of the pan.

Once the squash and potato are cooked, add them together with their cooking juices to the pan with the onion mixture, and give everything a good stir. If the garlic is soft enough, squeeze this out of the skins and into the pan too, but don't worry if they have become too crispy – just discard them, as the squash and potato will have taken on a deliciously subtle garlicky flavour while roasting.

Now add the coconut milk to the pan and allow to simmer very gently for a couple of minutes, uncovered. Remove the pan from the heat and purée the soup with a handheld electric blender until smooth. Alternatively, let cool for a few minutes, then transfer to a blender and blend until smooth. If the soup is too thick, feel free to add some hot water to loosen it slightly. Season to taste with salt and pepper.

Serve in small bowls, garnish with a little coriander/cilantro and drizzle with sesame oil.

Melon, tomato and feta salad

Perfect food for hot-weather dining. Sweet melon combined with juicy tomatoes and contrasted with salty feta, makes this a lovely dish. For a saltier contrast, substitute the feta with blue cheese and add sliced Parma ham. Serve with crusty bread to mop up every last drop of deliciousness.

½ Galia melon, peeled, deseeded and diced
½ cantaloupe melon, peeled, deseeded and diced
300 g/10 oz. tomatoes, sliced into wedges
2 tablespoons extra virgin olive oil
1 tablespoon sherry vinegar
2 tablespoons finely chopped fresh chives
freshly ground black pepper, to season
100 g/3½ oz. feta cheese, diced

Variation
50 g/2 oz. blue cheese, such as Stilton or Gorgonzola,
  crumbled into pieces
3 slices of Parma ham, shredded

SERVES 4

Toss together all the melon and tomato pieces with the oil, vinegar and chives in a serving dish. Season well with black pepper.

Gently mix in the feta cheese and serve at once.

Variation: Follow the instructions as above, replacing the feta with blue cheese. Stir in the shredded Parma ham and serve at once.

Chickpea, egg and potato salad

A hearty combination of flavours and textures, the nutty chickpeas are bound together by the slightly broken-up potato, hard-boiled/hard-cooked egg and oily dressing. This salad tastes best when it's still warm.

4 tablespoons olive oil

1 tablespoon white wine vinegar

1 tablespoon chopped fresh flat-leaf parsley

1 garlic clove, crushed

a 400-g/14-oz. can chickpeas

500 g/1 lb. new potatoes

a handful of pitted black olives

3 hard-boiled/hard-cooked eggs, peeled

a handful of fresh chives, chopped/snipped

salt and ground black pepper

SERVES 4

Make the vinaigrette dressing by whisking together the olive oil, white wine vinegar, parsley and garlic with a fork or a balloon whisk. Season with salt and pepper and set aside.

Boil the potatoes in salted water until tender. Drain, return to the warm pan and lightly squash with the back of a fork. Drain and rinse the chickpeas and mash one-third of them slightly, then mix with the whole chickpeas and the warm potatoes. Add the olives and vinaigrette and stir well.

Peel and chop the eggs and distribute them through the salad, taking care not to break them up too much. Sprinkle the chives over the top and serve immediately.

Quinoa and butter/lima bean salad with avocado

This satisfying Peruvian-inspired salad contains a pleasing combination
of textures and is enlivened by the lime–chilli/chile dressing.

125 g/½ cup quinoa
250 g/1¼ cups cooked, soaked
  dried butter/lima beans, or
  a 400-g/14-oz. can, drained
½ red onion, very finely diced
1 ripe avocado, stoned/pitted,
  peeled and diced
2 tomatoes, finely chopped
2 tablespoons fresh coriander/
  cilantro, roughly chopped

Vinaigrette
4 tablespoons olive oil
2 tablespoons freshly squeezed
  lime juice
1–2 fresh green chillies/chiles,
  deseeded and finely chopped
1 teaspoon sugar
salt and freshly ground
  black pepper, to season

SERVES 4–6

Wash the quinoa thoroughly, put in a saucepan and add 375 ml/
1½ cups of cold water. Cover the pan and bring to the boil, then
simmer for 20 minutes, by which time the water should have been
absorbed. Take the pan off the heat, fluff up the grains with a fork and
leave to cool.

Combine the butter/lima beans, red onion, avocado and tomatoes in
a large bowl. Stir in the cooked quinoa.

Make the vinaigrette by either whisking all the ingredients together
in a bowl with a fork or a balloon whisk, or by whizzing them up in
a small blender.

Stir the dressing into the bowl containing all of the other ingredients,
add the chopped coriander/cilantro and serve.

3 tablespoons olive oil

2 red onions, peeled and
    quartered

1 aubergine/eggplant, cut
    into chunks

1 courgette/zucchini, cut
    into chunks

1 sweet potato, cut into chunks

1 red (bell) pepper, deseeded
    and sliced into strips

a handful of cherry tomatoes

4 garlic cloves, unpeeled

250 g/9 oz. halloumi cheese,
    sliced into strips

140 g/2½ cups rocket/arugula

a handful of toasted pine nuts

salt and freshly ground
    black pepper, to season

Basil oil

a small handful of fresh
    basil leaves

100 ml/⅓ cup olive oil

SERVES 4

Roasted vegetable salad with grilled halloumi and basil oil

This fresh, colourful and satisfying salad will prove to be popular. Halloumi is a deliciously nutty Cypriot cheese but it must be served warm to enjoy it at its best.

Preheat the oven to 200°C (400°F) Gas 6.

Put the vegetables in a large roasting pan with the olive oil. Season well with salt and pepper. Roast in the preheated oven for 40–60 minutes, until the vegetables are soft and golden but still holding their shape.

To make the basil oil, bring a small saucepan of water to the boil. Put the basil leaves in the boiling water for just 10 seconds. Remove them and dip in a bowl of cold water to cool. Drain and dry the basil leaves, then put them in a food processor and set the motor running. Drizzle in the olive oil then strain the mixture into a bowl and set aside.

Lightly oil a stovetop a grill pan or frying pan/skillet and set over medium heat. Lay the strips of halloumi in the pan and cook until they turn golden brown, turning half way through cooking.

To assemble the salad, stir the rocket/arugula through the roasted vegetables. Spoon onto a serving plate and top with the halloumi. Drizzle with the basil oil and sprinkle over the pine nuts. Serve straight away.

Summer vegetable carpaccio

In this refreshing carpaccio, the nearly transparent slices of vegetable are enhanced with a tangy sour–sweet Asian dressing. You can use any firm vegetable – the key is to slice them thinly so that they can absorb the dressing and tenderize. Using a mandoline slicer will ensure neat, thin shavings. It makes a lovely light and attractive appetizer that is just right for summer entertaining.

5 large radishes
½ fennel bulb
1 large courgette/zucchini
½ red onion

Asian dressing
1 garlic clove
2 teaspoons finely chopped
*   fresh ginger*
1 tomato, peeled (see Tip,
*   page 49) and finely chopped*
1 tablespoon finely chopped
*   fresh mint*
1 tablespoon finely chopped
*   fresh coriander/cilantro*
grated zest of 1 lime and freshly
*   squeezed juice of ½*
3 tablespoons extra virgin
*   olive oil*
½ tablespoon rice wine or white
*   wine vinegar*
½ fresh red chilli/chile,
*   deseeded and very finely*
*   chopped*
1½ teaspoons white sugar
salt and freshly ground
*   black pepper, to season*

SERVES 4–6

Using a mandoline, vegetable peeler or very sharp knife, carefully slice the radishes, fennel, courgette/zucchini and red onion as thinly as possibly. Put the prepared vegetables in a non-reactive bowl, cover and set aside while you make the dressing.

To make the Asian dressing, simply put all of the ingredients with a pinch of salt and pepper in a small bowl and whisk with a fork until well combined.

To assemble, pour the dressing over the prepared vegetables and toss well to coat evenly. Use salad servers to arrange the salad on serving plates and serve immediately.

Prosciutto, artichoke, fig and Roquefort salad with balsamic dressing

This is an indulgent salad that combines the sweetness of fig with the saltiness of Prosciutto, and balances the flavours with creamy Roquefort. A simple balsamic dressing works here, as there are plenty of other flavours.

60 g/4 tablespoons butter

4 fresh figs (skin on), quartered

4 large handfuls of salad leaves of your choice, such as little Gem/Bibb lettuce

125 g/4¼ oz. Roquefort cheese, crumbled

16–20 cooked artichoke hearts, chopped (jarred marinated artichoke hearts are fine)

165 g/5½ oz. Prosciutto slices (about 20 average slices)

a small bunch of fresh basil leaves

salt and freshly ground black pepper, to season

Balsamic dressing

2 tablespoons olive oil

1 tablespoon balsamic vinegar

SERVES 4

Preheat the grill/broiler to high.

For the salad, rub a little butter on all the cut surfaces of the figs, put them on a baking sheet, cut-sides up, then pop them under the preheated grill/broiler for 6–8 minutes, turning once. Let them soften and start to brown, but don't let them shrivel up too much. Remove from the heat.

Meanwhile, make the dressing by combining the olive oil and vinegar in a bowl, seasoning with salt and pepper, and mixing well.

Dress the salad leaves with most of the dressing (reserving a little for drizzling on top) and divide between serving plates, then pop the Roquefort, grilled figs, artichokes, Prosciutto slices (see Tip) and basil leaves on top, dividing them evenly between each plate. Drizzle the salads with the remaining dressing and serve straight away.

Tip: It's always a shame to tear cured meat on top of salads because it doesn't look very pretty. However, remember that cured meat like Prosciutto doesn't cut very easily, so for the price of a little presentation, tear the Prosciutto into smaller pieces so it's distributed evenly for every mouthful.

Asian-style hot and sour salad with marinated tofu

This crunchy salad is perfect for a light lunch or as a small dish to serve as part of an Asian feast. You can use any fresh vegetables that you have to hand.

100 g/about 1 cup asparagus tips

100 g/about 1 cup mangetout/ snow peas

50 g/⅓ cup toasted cashews

100 g/2 cups beansprouts

100 g/3½ oz. cooked rice noodles (optional)

1 carrot, sliced into ribbons

1 tablespoon toasted sesame seeds, to serve

Marinated tofu

2 tablespoons sesame oil

1 tablespoon dark soy sauce or tamari

½ fresh red chilli/chile, finely chopped

1 teaspoon grated fresh ginger

grated zest and freshly squeezed juice of ½ lime

½ teaspoon sugar

200 g/7 oz. tofu

Asian dressing

½ teaspoon salt

2 teaspoons sugar

grated zest and freshly squeezed juice of 1 lime

1 teaspoon white wine vinegar

½ fresh red chilli/chile

SERVES 4

For the marinated tofu, put all of the ingredients except the tofu in a bowl and stir until well combined. Put the tofu in a separate bowl, pour the marinade over it and set aside for 30 minutes.

Bring a saucepan of water to the boil and cook the asparagus and mangetout/snow peas for 3 minutes, until they soften slightly but still have a crunch to them. Remove from the boiling water and put into a bowl of ice-cold water to stop the cooking process. Drain, then slice in half lengthways and put them in a serving bowl. Add the cashews.

Put all of the dressing ingredients into a bowl and stir until well combined. Add the rest of the salad ingredients to the serving bowl, pour over the dressing and toss to coat the salad. Crumble the marinated tofu over the top and sprinkle with sesame seeds.

Meat and poultry

Make-ahead pâtés and terrines can ease last-minute time pressures, super-savoury cured meats come into their own when served as an appetizer — bringing maximum flavour with the minimum of fuss — and the spicy and moreish meat treats included here won't disappoint either.

Chicken liver pâté

Contrary to what you might think, pâté is not hard to make. The foundation of a simple chicken liver pâté can also be a great basis for some fun with additional flavours and ingredients. Here's a classic combination to get you started.

45 g/3½ tablespoons butter

2 shallots, chopped

1 garlic clove, chopped

75 g/3 oz. pork belly (rind removed), diced

200 g/7 oz. chicken livers, chopped

a pinch of freshly chopped thyme, plus extra to decorate

1 tablespoon brandy

2 bay leaves

1 teaspoon freshly squeezed lemon juice

salt and freshly ground black pepper, to season

black and pink peppercorns, to decorate

wholemeal/whole-wheat crispbreads or oatcakes (home-baked if possible) and fig chutney, to serve

SERVES 4

Heat 20 g/generous 1 tablespoon of the butter in a frying pan/skillet over a medium heat, until melted. Add the shallots and garlic and fry on their own for 1 minute. Add the pork belly, chicken livers, thyme and brandy, season with salt and pepper, and stir. Put the bay leaves on top and let them soften, if you are using dried ones. Cook, stirring regularly for 10 minutes, until everything is browned and the chicken livers are cooked through.

Remove from the heat and let cool until the mixture is warm, not hot – don't let it cool completely, otherwise the ingredients will dry out. Remove and discard the bay leaves.

Put the mixture into a food processor (don't wash the pan yet), add a squeeze of lemon juice and whizz; how much depends on how coarse you like it. Pulse for a short time to keep some chunks, or if you like it quite smooth, process until the mixture sticks to the sides. Spoon the mixture into a dish (or into separate ramekins) and level the surface so that the melted butter can go on top.

In the same frying pan/skillet you were using before, melt the remaining butter over a medium heat, until it starts to bubble, then remove from the heat and pour over the top of the pâté. Decorate with a little extra thyme and some black and pink peppercorns. Move the pâté to the refrigerator and the butter will set in about 1 hour.

Serve with wholemeal/whole-wheat crispbreads or home-baked oatcakes, plus a little fig chutney to sweeten, if you like.

Tip: The pâté will keep in the fridge for 1 week, if the butter is unbroken on the top. Eat within 3 days once you have dipped through the surface. You can freeze the pâté in balls wrapped in clingfilm/plastic wrap (without the melted butter topping) and slowly defrost (do not reheat nor microwave). Once defrosted, you can transfer to ramekins and add the melted butter to the top.

Pâté de campagne

This is not technically a pâté, but is similar as it is served like one. Make it a day ahead, and let it come to room temperature for 20–30 minutes before serving.

30 g/2 tablespoons butter

2 tablespoons brandy

4 shallots, finely chopped

1 garlic clove, finely chopped

1 egg

4 tablespoons double/heavy cream

½ teaspoon Dijon mustard

a pinch of fresh thyme leaves

400 g/14 oz. pork loin or shoulder (as much fat removed as possible), trimmed and cut into 1-cm/ ½-inch cubes

6 slices Prosciutto

100 g/3½ oz. ham hock, chopped (optional)

1 hard-boiled/hard-cooked egg, peeled (optional)

salt and freshly ground black pepper, to season

To serve (optional)

mixed pickles

crispbreads

a 20 x 10-cm/8 x 4-inch loaf pan, greased

SERVES 4

Preheat the oven to 180°C (350°F) Gas 4.

Melt the butter in a frying pan/skillet over a medium heat, then add the brandy. Let it boil and reduce for a minute, then add the shallots and garlic. Once those have softened, remove the frying pan/skillet from the heat and let cool.

In a bowl, beat the egg and then stir in the cream, mustard and thyme, and season with salt and pepper. Add the pork, then stir in the cooled shallot mixture and any juices from the pan.

Lay the slices of Prosciutto across the bottom and up the sides of the prepared loaf pan so that they line it. Leave a small gap between the slices to make the loaf easier to slice once it's cooked and then chilled. Spoon half of the pork mixture into the pan and then sprinkle the ham hock pieces across the middle, if using. If you wish, place a peeled hard-boiled/hard-cooked egg in the middle – it looks attractive when sliced.

Spoon the remaining pork mixture on top and then fold the ends of the Prosciutto across the top if the slices are longer than the inside surface of the loaf pan. Cover the pan tightly with foil. Take a larger roasting dish and put 2.5 cm/1 inch of water in the bottom to create a water bath. Lower the loaf pan into the water and cook in the preheated oven for 1 hour, until the mixture around the meat has thickened and the meat is firm to the touch. Remove the loaf pan from the water bath and let cool for 30 minutes.

Move to the fridge to finish setting, ideally overnight since the pâté will take a good few hours to set properly.

To serve, just run a knife around the edge of the loaf to release it from the sides of the pan, then turn it out onto a board to slice. Enjoy with pickles and crispbreads.

Pork rillettes

Rillettes are like a pâté with a bit more texture, because the meat is shredded, rather than puréed. Best served at room temperature with some Melba toast or crispbread, this special and flavourful appetizer or canapé is very easy to make.

200 g/7 oz. pork belly (rind removed), trimmed and diced
1 tablespoon sea salt
30 g/2 tablespoons butter
1 garlic clove, finely chopped
a small pinch of ground mace
1 bay leaf
a pinch of freshly chopped or dried parsley
50 ml/scant ¼ cup dry white wine
150 ml/⅔ cup chicken stock
salt and freshly ground black pepper, to season
freshly squeezed lemon juice, freshly chopped parsley and Melba toast, to serve

SERVES 2

Put the pork belly in a non-metallic container and sprinkle the sea salt over the top. Massage the salt into the meat, then cover tightly and refrigerate for 1–2 hours. Rinse and dry the pork – the salt should have already drawn some of the moisture out of it, but you don't want to draw out too much because you're going to slow-cook it, which will benefit from keeping the fat.

Melt the butter in a saucepan over a medium heat, then add the pork, garlic, mace, bay leaf and parsley, and season with salt and pepper. Cook, stirring often, to slightly brown the pork and coat it in the seasoning, then add the white wine and increase the heat to high for 1–2 minutes to reduce the wine. Pour in the chicken stock.

Turn the heat down to very low and put a lid on the pan. Leave it cooking gently for 1¼ hours. At this stage, press one of the pork pieces with a fork and if it starts to fall apart, it's had long enough, but it's likely that it'll need a little longer. If the mixture is starting to dry out and stick to the bottom of the pan, add another splash of chicken stock – about 50 ml/scant ¼ cup. Replace the lid and leave to cook gently for another 20–30 minutes, until the meat is falling apart.

Remove from the heat and leave to cool. Discard the bay leaf. When cool enough to touch, pull the meat apart and mix it really well with your fingers. The fat should have melted, but take out and discard any large pieces.

Transfer the pork to a container or individual ramekins and chill in the fridge for at least 1 hour to set. The texture of shredded meat is best at room temperature as it allows the flavour to come through really well, so bring it out of the fridge about 30 minutes before serving. Add a squeeze of lemon juice, an extra crack of black pepper and a sprinkling of freshly chopped parsley.

Tip: This recipe also works well with duck, pheasant, beef (diced sirloin or rib-eye steak) and venison. If using venison, which is very lean, add 100 g/3¼ oz. rindless pork belly for extra flavour.

1 kg/3 lbs. minced/ground lamb
1½ teaspoons ground cumin
1½ teaspoons smoked sweet
    paprika
1 teaspoon ground allspice
1 teaspoon chilli powder
150 g/1 cup finely diced red
    onion
25 g/½ cup fresh flat-leaf
    parsley, finely chopped
40 g/¾ cup fresh coriander/
    cilantro, finely chopped,
    plus extra to serve
freshly squeezed juice and
    grated zest of 1 lemon, plus
    wedges to serve
3 large eggs
1 teaspoon sea salt
60 ml/¼ cup sunflower oil,
    for frying

Tahini yogurt dip
250 ml/1 cup Greek yogurt
25 ml/2 tablespoons tahini
    paste
2 tablespoons freshly squeezed
    lemon juice
10 g/¼ cup mint, finely
    chopped
¼ cucumber, grated
1 garlic clove, crushed
½ teaspoon sea salt

To serve
fresh coriander/cilantro,
    roughly chopped
lemon wedges

30 x 15-cm/6-inch wooden
    skewers, soaked in water
    for at least 30 minutes

**MAKES 30 SKEWERS
AND SERVES 10–15**

Lamb koftes with a tahini yogurt dip

Mini skewers of succulent lamb make great party canapés, especially as they can be prepared in advance. Serve with a dip of cooling yogurt on the side.

To make the koftes, place all the ingredients except the oil in a large mixing bowl and mix everything together using your hands.

Shape the kofte mixture around the soaked skewers (about 45–50 g/ 1½–2 oz. per skewer) in a sausage shape and press firmly together. Transfer to a baking sheet, cover with clingfilm/plastic wrap and set in the fridge for at least 2 hours, or preferably overnight, to firm up.

Preheat the oven to 180°C (350°F) Gas 4.

Heat the sunflower oil in a large frying pan/skillet set over a medium-high heat. Add the koftes in batches and cook for about 4 minutes, turning them until golden brown all over. Transfer to a clean baking sheet while you cook the remaining koftes in the same way, adding more oil to the pan each time if necessary.

When all the koftes have been fried, put the baking sheet in the preheated oven for 5 minutes to cook through.

To make the tahini yogurt dip, mix all the ingredients together and set aside.

Serve the koftes on a platter scattered with chopped coriander/ cilantro, with lemon wedges and the tahini yogurt dip on the side.

Parma ham and melon

This is such a classic appetizer but you can forgive what it lacks in imagination and flair, since it gains in everyone still having plenty of room for a lovely big main course/entrée. So don't knock it until you've welcomed seconds of pudding, when you'll be grateful that you chose it!

8 slices Parma ham
½ melon, peeled, deseeded and sliced into thin slices
freshly squeezed lime juice
freshly ground black pepper, to season

SERVES 4

Divide the ham and melon evenly between the serving plates. Either place the Parma ham and melon neatly on the plate next to each other or wrap the Parma ham around the slices of melon. Squeeze lime juice over the top of each serving and sprinkle with pepper.

Parma ham and grapefruit

This alternative to the classic ham-and-melon combo above is arguably even nicer. Serve the grapefruit segments and Parma ham next to each other, rather than wrapping the Parma ham around the grapefruit. This is so people can put just the right balance of the sour and salty on their forks to suit their own tastebuds.

8 white grapefruit segments
8 pink grapefruit segments
8 tablespoons sloe gin (or other fruit liqueur)
8 slices Parma ham

SERVES 4

Put the grapefruit segments into a bowl, pour over the sloe gin and leave to soak for at least 1 hour, but ideally for 3–4 hours.

Serve with the Parma ham, allowing 4 grapefruit segments (plus some sloe gin) and 2 slices of Parma ham per serving.

Beef empañadas with Texan hot sauce

These delicious Spanish pastry parcels filled with herbed meat are perfect to hand around at parties. Bite-size and dipped in hot sauce, they are hard to resist.

2 tablespoons olive oil

½ white onion, finely diced

2 garlic cloves, finely chopped

1 jalapeño chilli/chile, diced

225 g/8 oz. minced/ground beef

2 teaspoons each of dried marjoram and dried oregano

60 ml/¼ cup black olive tapenade

1 teaspoon sweet paprika

125 ml/½ cup red wine

1 egg, lightly beaten

salt and freshly ground black pepper, to season

Pastry

250 g/2 cups plain/all-purpose flour

175 g/1½ sticks cold butter, cubed

a pinch of sea salt

1 egg, lightly beaten

5 tablespoons iced water

Texan hot sauce

16 fresh red jalapeño chillies/ chiles

14 garlic cloves, bashed

3 tablespoons vegetable oil

1 tablespoon smoked paprika

2 tablespoons ancho chillies/ chiles in adobo sauce

85 g/¼ cup clear honey

60 ml/¼ cup rice wine vinegar

55 g/¼ cup dark brown sugar

a 9-cm/3½-inch cookie cutter

a baking sheet lined with baking parchment

MAKES 28

First make the pastry. Put the flour, butter and salt in a food processor and pulse until it resembles breadcrumbs. Add the egg and pulse to combine. With the motor running, add the iced water and process until the pastry comes together. Turn out onto a lightly floured surface and knead into a disc. Cover with clingfilm/plastic wrap and refrigerate for 30 minutes.

Next make the Texan hot sauce. Preheat the oven to 375°F (190°C) Gas 5. Put the jalapeños (stems removed) and garlic in a baking dish, drizzle with the oil and toss. Roast for 25–30 minutes, stirring halfway through. Remove from the oven and leave to cool before putting in a food processor. Add the paprika, ancho chiles, honey, vinegar, sugar and a little water, then blend until smooth. Pour the mixture into a non-reactive pan and bring to a boil. Reduce the heat and simmer for 15 minutes until the colour deepens. Set aside until ready to serve.

When you are ready to assemble and cook the empañadas, preheat the oven to 210°C (425°F) Gas 7.

Heat the olive oil in a frying pan/skillet over medium–high heat, add the onion, garlic and jalapeño, and cook for 5 minutes until golden brown. Add the beef, marjoram, oregano, olive tapenade and paprika, and stir. Pour in the wine and cook for 8 minutes, stirring occasionally. Season with salt and pepper, remove the pan from the heat, and cool.

Roll out the chilled pastry as thinly as possible on a lightly floured surface, and cut rounds of pastry with the cookie cutter. Gather the leftover pastry and repeat until all the pastry is used up. Place a teaspoon of the filling in the middle of each round. Fold over and seal the edges with a fork. Arrange on the prepared baking sheet and brush with the beaten egg.

Bake in the preheated oven for 15 minutes until golden brown. Sprinkle with salt and serve the empañadas with Texan hot sauce on the side. Leftover sauce can be stored in an airtight container and kept in the fridge for up to 1 week.

Hot Prosciutto parcels stuffed with goat's cheese and fresh basil

These tasty little parcels can be served as a canapé, in groups of three for an appetizer, or on top of a salad.

12 slices Prosciutto
125 g/generous ½ cup soft
    goat's cheese
24 fresh basil leaves
freshly ground black pepper,
    to season
salad leaves, to serve

MAKES 12

For each Prosciutto parcel, lay a slice of Prosciutto flat and put a heaped teaspoon of the goat's cheese at one end. Place 2 basil leaves on top and sprinkle with a pinch of pepper. Fold the Prosciutto over so that the goat's cheese is wrapped tightly inside. Repeat to make 12 Prosciutto parcels in total.

Heat a dry frying pan/skillet (there's no need for oil if it's non-stick) or grill pan over a medium heat, until hot. Put the Prosciutto parcels in the hot pan and cook for about 2 minutes on each side.

Remove from the heat and let cool slightly to serve as finger food or put on top of a bed of salad leaves.

Variations: You can use coppa or Serrano ham instead of Prosciutto, if you prefer. If you're not a fan of goat's cheese, this recipe also works well with halloumi. Just slice the halloumi, pop it under a preheated hot grill/broiler for 4–5 minutes first until it's lightly tinged brown and then wrap the halloumi in the Prosciutto slices with either the basil or fresh parsley, before cooking the parcels as above. Halloumi is a richer cheese than goat's cheese, so you could add a squeeze of lemon juice or some balsamic vinegar on top, if you like.

Steak tartare with mustard cheese toasts

Steak tartare embodies the best bits of a burger – the grunt of meat, the lick of ketchup and the salty punch of pickle. And while the mustard cheese melt is not the standard accompaniment to steak tartare, it still makes a perfect sidekick.

2 tablespoons Dijon mustard

4 anchovy fillets, finely diced

2 tablespoons ketchup

1 tablespoon Worcestershire
    sauce

1 small onion, finely chopped

2 tablespoons capers, finely
    chopped

2 tablespoons cornichons,
    finely chopped

2 tablespoons fresh flat leaf
    parsley, finely chopped

500 g/1 lb. 2 oz. beef sirloin,
    very finely diced (don't use
    a food processor)

Tabasco, to taste

4 quail egg yolks (or 2 ordinary
    egg yolks)

salt and freshly ground black
    pepper, to season

rocket/arugula, to serve

Mustard cheese toasts

2 tablespoons butter, melted

1 tablespoon hot English
    mustard

75 g/³/4 cup grated Cheddar
    cheese

1 baguette, sliced into 1-cm/
    ½-inch slices

SERVES 4

Put the Dijon mustard, anchovies, ketchup and Worcestershire sauce in a large bowl and whisk. Add the onion, capers, cornichons and parsley.

Add the chopped beef to the bowl and mix well using a spoon. Season with salt, pepper and Tabasco to taste. Divide the meat evenly between 4 chilled dinner plates.

Wash the quail egg shells well. Separate the quail eggs and nestle the yolks in half-shells on top of the steak tartare, for guests to mix as they like. (If you don't have quail eggs, use 2 egg yolks and whisk them with the mustard and ketchup mixture).

To make the mustard cheese toasts, preheat the grill/broiler to high. Combine the melted butter and English mustard and brush the mixture over the baguette slices. Top with cheese and grill/broil for 5 minutes, until the tops are melted and bubbly.

Serve with the steak tartare and rocket/arugula on the side.

Fish and seafood

Whether served fresh and light with a citrusy tang,
or dusted with golden breadcrumbs, fish is an endlessly
versatile ingredient. Choose a light fish ceviche for
sophisticated summer dining or opt for flaky pastry-
enrobed luxury seafood for a special occasion meal.

Seafood cocktails

Often the classic retro dishes are the best, and this is one such example. Use a selection of different prawns/shrimp to make this a more sophisticated number. If you're feeling glam, add some cooked chopped lobster or crayfish tails to the mix.

12 cherry tomatoes, roughly
    chopped
4 spring onions/scallions,
    trimmed and thinly sliced
1 fresh red chilli/chile,
    deseeded and finely chopped
1 garlic clove, crushed
freshly squeezed juice of 1 lime
400 g/14 oz. cooked and peeled
    prawns/shrimp in assorted
    sizes
2 tablespoons freshly chopped
    coriander/cilantro
a few drops of Tabasco
1 ripe avocado
½ iceberg lettuce, shredded
salt and freshly ground black
    pepper, to season
lime wedges, to serve

4–6 individual glass dishes

SERVES 4–6

Put the tomatoes, spring onions/scallions and chilli/chile in a bowl with the crushed garlic and freshly squeezed lime juice and mix well.

Add the prawns/shrimp, chopped coriander/cilantro, a shake of Tabasco and season well with salt and black pepper.

Cover and set aside to marinate for 10 minutes.

Peel and dice the avocado and gently stir it into the prawn/shrimp mixture. Arrange a handful of shredded lettuce in each serving dish, spoon the prawn/shrimp mixture over the top and serve immediately with extra lime wedges for squeezing.

Salt and pepper squid with lime aïoli

These deliciously crispy squid pieces taste so good because they're cooked in lots of oil, but get the oil hot enough and they will be surprisingly light, not at all greasy or heavy. Serve with a tangy lime aioli on the side for dipping.

600 g/1¼ lb. squid, cleaned

75 g/½ cup rice flour or cornflour/cornstarch

1 teaspoon Chinese five-spice

1 teaspoon sea salt

1 teaspoon freshly ground white or black pepper

vegetable oil, for frying

1 long red chilli/chile, deseeded and thinly sliced

20 g/scant ½ cup chopped coriander/cilantro

lime wedges, for squeezing

Lime aïoli

2 very fresh egg yolks

1 garlic clove, crushed

2 teaspoons Dijon mustard

250 ml/1 cup olive oil

freshly squeezed juice and grated zest of 1 lime

salt and freshly ground black pepper, to season

SERVES 4–6

Begin by preparing the lime aïoli. Put the egg yolks, garlic and mustard in a food processor and blitz to a paste. With the motor still running very slowly, add the oil in a slow, steady drizzle until it forms a thick sauce. Stir in the lime juice, zest and 2 tablespoons of water. Season with salt and pepper to taste, then cover and set in the fridge until you are ready to serve.

To prepare the squid, cut down the 'seam' of the squid so it opens out flat. Pat dry with paper towels. Score the inside with a cross-hatch pattern then slice the squid lengthways into 2-cm/¾-inch strips.

Mix the rice flour or cornflour/cornstarch, Chinese five-spice, salt and pepper together in a shallow dish or plate. Toss all the squid pieces in the seasoned flour to coat and set aside.

Pour vegetable oil into a frying pan/skillet or wok to a depth of about 2.5 cm/1 inch. Set over a high heat and bring to a smoking heat. Test whether it is hot enough to fry the squid by flicking some flour into the oil – it should sizzle vigorously.

Shake off any excess flour from the squid strips and fry in the hot oil in batches for 2–3 minutes, until lightly golden brown.

Remove the squid from the oil with a slotted spoon and drain on paper towels, while you cook the remaining strips in the same way. When all the squid is cooked, transfer to a large mixing bowl.

Add the sliced chilli/chile and chopped coriander/cilantro and toss the squid to coat. Heap the squid onto a serving platter garnished with lime wedges and lime aïoli on the side to dip into.

Scallop and black pudding puffs

The scallops for this luxury appetizer should be about the same width as the sliced black pudding. You can slice a larger black pudding and use a pastry cutter to stamp out rounds to fit. Freeze any remaining pastry for up to 3 months.

6 medium-size fresh scallops

freshly squeezed juice of
1 lemon

500-g/17-oz package
ready-made puff pastry

6 x 1-cm/½-inch slices cut
from a small 170 g/6 oz.
black pudding or chorizo
sausage

1 egg, beaten with a pinch of
salt, to glaze

Furikake (Japanese seaweed
and sesame seasoning)

salt and freshly ground
black pepper, to season

Basil and sun-dried tomato
butter

175 g/1½ sticks unsalted butter

3 tablespoons finely shredded
fresh basil

6 sun-dried tomatoes in oil,
drained and finely sliced

2 tablespoons grated Parmesan

a 6-hole muffin pan, greased

a 12-cm/5-inch round plain
pastry cutter

a 10-cm/4-inch round plain
pastry cutter

a 10-cm/4-inch round fluted
pastry cutter

MAKES 6

First, make the basil and sun-dried tomato butter. Beat the butter until really soft, then beat in the basil, tomatoes and Parmesan. Spoon onto a sheet of clingfilm/plastic wrap and roll up into a log, twisting the ends. Chill for at least an hour until hard.

Preheat the oven to 220ºC (425ºF) Gas 7.

Remove the roe (if any) from the scallops and discard or freeze for use another time. Pull off the little hard muscle found on the scallop opposite the roe and remove any membrane. Put the scallops in a bowl, season with salt and pepper and toss with the lemon juice.

On a lightly floured surface, roll out the puff pastry to rectangles measuring approximately 35 x 27 cm/14 x 11 inches. Using the large round cutter, stamp out 6 rounds from one rectangle and use them to line the muffin-pan holes. Use the smaller plain cutter to stamp out 6 rounds from the other rectangle for the tops and set aside.

Cut 12 slices of flavoured butter from the roll. Lay a slice of black pudding in the base of each puff and top with a slice of butter, then with a whole scallop and then with another slice of butter. Dampen the edges with the beaten egg, then top with the remaining pastry rounds and seal.

Trim by using the small fluted cutter to stamp over each pie, being careful that they are still well sealed. Make a tiny steam hole in the top of each puff, brush with beaten egg and sprinkle with the Furikake. Bake in the preheated oven for 10–13 minutes until puffed and golden. Serve immediately.

Thai fishcakes with nahm jim dipping sauce

These bite-size fishcakes are full of fresh Asian flavours and make a wonderfully different first course, especially if the rest of the meal has a spicy theme. The sour sweet flavour of the accompanying dipping sauce contrasts beautifully.

500 g/1¼ lbs. haddock or other
   white fish, roughly chopped
2 fresh red chillies/chiles,
   roughly chopped
3 spring onions/scallions,
   roughly chopped
5 lime leaves, chopped
2 garlic cloves, roughly chopped
a 2-cm/¾-inch piece of fresh
   ginger, peeled and chopped
1 tablespoon fish sauce
200 g/¾ cup prawns/shrimp,
   peeled and chopped
50 g/1 cup coriander/cilantro,
   finely chopped, plus extra
   to garnish
vegetable oil, for frying

Nahm jim
1 garlic clove
2 coriander roots/cilantro
   roots, roughly chopped
3 red chillies/chiles, roughly
   chopped
a 2-cm/¾-inch piece of ginger,
   peeled and roughly chopped
3 tablespoons palm sugar
3 tablespoons fish sauce
125 ml/½ cup freshly squeezed
   lime juice

2 baking sheets, 1 greased
   and lined with baking
   parchment

MAKES 12

Put 100 g/3½ oz. of the fish, the chillies/chiles, spring onions/scallions, lime leaves, garlic, ginger and fish sauce in a large mixing bowl and stir well to combine. Blitz to a paste consistency using a handheld electric blender or in a food processor. This paste is used to bind the fishcakes.

Mix the paste with the remaining fish, prawns/shrimp and coriander/cilantro. Using your hands, form 12 round patties, each about 75 g/3 oz. Arrange the fishcakes on the unlined baking sheet, cover with clingfilm/plastic wrap and set in the fridge to firm up. As there is no egg to bind the mixture in this recipe, they need at least 2 hours in the fridge to firm up. Omitting the egg gives the fishcakes a lighter texture.

When ready to serve, preheat the oven to 180ºC (350ºF) Gas 4 and cover the bottom of a non-stick frying pan/skillet with vegetable oil, about ½-cm/¼-inch deep. Sear the fishcakes in batches for 2 minutes on each side until lightly golden. Transfer to the lined baking sheet while you cook the remaining fishcakes in the same way. When all the fishcakes are seared, transfer to the preheated oven for another 3 minutes to cook through.

To make the nahm jim, use a mortar in a pestle to pound the garlic, coriander/cilantro roots, chillies/chiles and ginger to a rough paste. Add the palm sugar, fish sauce and lime juice and mix thoroughly. Add more palm sugar, lime or fish sauce if necessary to get the desired balance of sweet, sour and salty.

Serve the fishcakes hot with the nahm jim on the side, garnished with fresh coriander/cilantro.

Chilli/chile-marinated salmon gravadlax

If you have a fondness for the cured and pickled fish common in Scandinavian cuisine you will be pleased to discover that curing fish is not as much of a dark art as you might think. On the contrary, it is a surprisingly simple process.

2 small–medium whole
    salmon fillets, skin on and
    pin-boned
grated zest and freshly
    squeezed juice of 1 lemon
a large bunch of fresh dill,
    chopped
brown toast, to serve
very finely grated fresh
    horseradish, to serve

Chilli/chile-infused vodka
75 ml/¹⁄₃ cup vodka
1–2 red bird's eye
    chillies/chiles, chopped

Cure
150 g/¹⁄₃ cup sea salt flakes
175 g/scant cup sugar
3 tablespoons mixed
    peppercorns, freshly and
    coarsely ground

a small glass jar with an
    airtight lid
a glass or other non-metallic
    dish large enough to hold
    the salmon fillets one on
    top of the other
a rigid board that will fit
    inside the dish

MAKES 20 SERVINGS

First make the chilli-infused vodka. Pour the vodka into a small jar and add the chopped chillies. Tightly seal and set aside in a warm place for 24 hours. Give the jar a shake whenever you are passing. After this period, strain the infused vodka into a small cup or jar and set aside until ready to use.

To make the cure, mix the salt, sugar and peppercorns in a small bowl. Lay a large sheet of clingfilm/plastic wrap (it will need to be large enough to wrap around the salmon fillets) over a dish large enough to take the salmon fillets. Place one fillet, skin side down, on the clingfilm/plastic wrap. Spread half the cure mixture over the surface of the salmon. Evenly distribute half the lemon zest over the cure, then cover with the dill. Sprinkle the infused vodka over the fillet and cover with the rest of the cure mixture. Place the second fillet, skin-side up, on the first fillet.

Wrap the clingfilm/plastic wrap tightly around the salmon. On top of this place a rigid board and weight down with a few heavy cans or jars. Refrigerate for 24 hours.

After this period, remove the dish from the fridge, unwrap the fillets and baste with the liquid that has been drawn out from the salmon. Re-wrap, flip over in the dish, weigh it down as before and refrigerate for 24 hours more.

Remove the salmon from its wrapping, separate the fillets and scrape away any excess cure/lemon/dill mixture. Using a sharp knife, carefully remove the skin. Trim away any brown bits from the skin side of the fillet. Slice very thinly at an oblique angle and serve on brown toast with a dressing of grated horseradish and a squeeze of lemon juice.

West Coast crab cakes

Crab cakes are best made using fresh crabmeat, but if it is not in season, you can use good-quality canned crabmeat instead. Serve with herbed yogurt and citrus wedges for extra zing.

450 g/1 lb. fresh crabmeat
grated zest and freshly
    squeezed juice of 1 lemon
180 g/¾ cup fresh corn kernels
2 spring onions/scallions,
    finely chopped
2 eggs, lightly beaten
1 jalapeño chilli/chile, finely
    chopped
1½ tablespoons preserved
    lemons, finely chopped
    (optional)
80 g/2 cups fresh or Panko
    breadcrumbs
salt and cracked black pepper,
    to season
vegetable oil, for frying

To serve
lime halves, for squeezing
plain yogurt
fresh green herbs, chopped

MAKES 12

Mix together the crabmeat, lemon zest and juice, corn, spring onions/scallions, half of the beaten egg, chilli/chile, and pickled kaffir limes in a large mixing bowl. Season with salt and pepper.

For the coating, put the remaining beaten egg in a small, shallow bowl and the breadcrumbs on a plate. Shape a large tablespoon of the crab mixture into 12 cakes with your hands. Dip each cake into the egg, then roll in the breadcrumbs.

Heat a frying pan/skillet over medium–high heat and drizzle with a little vegetable oil. Working in batches, fry the crab cakes for 4 minutes on each side until golden brown, crispy and cooked through. Transfer to a warm serving platter and serve with a squeeze of fresh lime and thick, creamy natural set yogurt sprinkled with chopped green herbs.

Crab empañadas

These little pies are best made with sweet fresh crabmeat. Frozen crabmeat is too wet and lacks flavour, so at a pinch use canned crabmeat instead. Crab marries well with chilli/chile; Peppadews from South Africa are perfect.

175 g/6 oz. fresh white crabmeat

6 spring onions/scallions, chopped

3 Peppadew peppers, finely diced or minced

2 tablespoons sour cream or crème fraîche, plus 1–2 tablespoons extra, to glaze (optional)

a dash of Green Jalapeño Tabasco, plus extra, to glaze (optional)

500-g/17-oz packet ready-made puff pastry

1 tablespoon black onion seeds (kalonji), to sprinkle

salt and freshly ground black pepper, to season

an 8-cm/3-inch round pastry cutter

a baking sheet lined with baking parchment

MAKES 10

Preheat the oven to 400°C (200°F) Gas 6.

Mix the crabmeat, spring onions/scallions, peppers, sour cream or crème fraîche and the Tabasco in a medium-size bowl, then taste and season with salt and pepper. Set aside.

On a lightly floured surface, roll out the pastry to a thickness of 3–5 mm/⅛–¼ inch. Using the pastry cutter, stamp out 10 circles of pastry. Remove and discard the trimmings.

Place teaspoonfuls of the crab mixture into the centre of each pastry circle, dampen the edges with a little water and fold each in half. Pinch the edges to seal, then use a fork or the end of a spoon to make a decorative edge. Arrange the empañadas about 5 cm/2 inches apart on the prepared baking sheet.

The empañadas can be left unglazed or, at this point, can be brushed with 1–2 tablespoons of sour cream mixed with 2 teaspoons water, a pinch of salt and a dash of Tabasco. Very lightly sprinkle with black onion seeds.

It is better to bake these immediately as the mixture is quite wet and could make the pastry go soggy. Bake in the preheated oven for about 12 minutes until puffed and golden.

Enjoy warm or cold.

Brazilian black-eyed bean and shrimp fritters

These fritters are known as 'acarajé' in Brazil, and are a popular snack of the Bahia region in the north of the country. They make an interesting appetizer and are almost certainly something your guests won't have tried before!

200 g/1 cup dried black-eyed beans/peas, soaked overnight and drained

1 onion, chopped

2 fresh chillies/chiles, red or green, chopped

½ teaspoon fish sauce

1 egg white, lightly beaten

1 teaspoon salt

125 g/4 oz. peeled prawns/shrimp, chopped

vegetable oil, for frying

Salsa

1 red onion, finely chopped

1 tomato, peeled (see Tip page 49) and chopped

1 garlic clove, finely chopped

2 tablespoons olive oil

1 tablespoon freshly squeezed lime juice

1 fresh chilli/chile, green or red, finely chopped

1 tablespoon chopped fresh coriander/cilantro

salt and freshly ground black pepper, to season

MAKES ABOUT 24

Put the black-eyed beans/peas in a saucepan, cover with 3 times their volume of water and bring to the boil. Simmer for 2 minutes, then take the pan off the heat and leave the beans/peas to soak in the water for 4 hours. Drain off the water and put the beans/peas into a food processor. Pulse briefly to break the skins, then add enough water to cover them and pulse again – some will break up, but don't worry about this. Transfer the beans/peas and water to a large bowl and put in the sink. Rub the beans/peas vigorously with your fingers to loosen the skins, then put the bowl under cold running water, swishing the beans around so that the skins rise to the surface and can be skimmed off and discarded. Drain the beans/peas thoroughly when most of the skins have been removed.

In a food processor, blend the beans/peas, onion, chillies/chiles, fish sauce, egg white and salt with 125 ml/½ cup of water to make a paste. Transfer the mixture to a bowl, then add the chopped prawns/shrimp and mix well to incorporate them. Cover and leave this batter in the fridge for 1 hour.

Mix all of the salsa ingredients together in a bowl and set aside.

Heat the oil in a saucepan – it should be at least 5 cm/2 inches. deep so that the fritters are covered. When the oil is hot, slip spoonfuls of the batter into the hot oil and fry in batches until golden brown on all sides, making sure they are fully cooked through.

Drain on paper towels and serve hot with the salsa.

Spicy coconut ceviche

This dish is known as 'kokoda' and is a coconut ceviche popular in Fiji and the Pacific. The fish is 'cooked' by the citrus, then softened by the coconut milk. There's chilli/chile for warmth and tomato and onion for freshness. It is the perfect recipe for days when languor or disinclination prohibit taxing activities such as cooking. Serve it in lettuce cups for a light and unusual summer appetizer.

250 g/8 oz. fresh mahi-mahi, snapper or sea bass, skinned and pin-boned
freshly squeezed juice of 1 lime
2 spring onions/scallions, sliced
½ green chilli/chile, thinly sliced
1 Roma tomato, seeds removed, chopped into small dice
90 ml/⅓ cup coconut milk
1 head iceberg or romaine lettuce
salt, to sprinkle
lime wedges, to serve

SERVES 4

Cut the fish into 1-cm/¾-inch dice and sprinkle with salt. Add the lime juice and stir thoroughly so that the lime juice 'cooks' the fish. Cover and marinate for 30 minutes in the fridge.

Toss the fish, then return to the fridge for another 30 minutes.

Combine the fish with the spring onions/scallions, chilli/chile and tomato. Strain off some of the juices that will have gathered at the bottom.

Transfer to a bowl, pour the coconut milk over the top and stir to combine. Serve as soon as possible and keep the mixture covered and refrigerated up to the point of serving.

Spoon the ceviche into lettuce leaf cups and serve with lime wedges on the side for squeezing.

Vietnamese rice paper rolls

Rice paper wrappers or 'bánh tráng' should not be confused with wonton wrappers. You'll find then in Asian supermarkets. If you don't have time to make the dipping sauce, serve these light, fresh, herb-filled rolls with hoisin sauce.

40 g/1½ oz. rice vermicelli
    noodles
¼ cucumber, peeled
1 carrot, peeled
1 head baby gem or baby
    romaine lettuce
a handful of beansprouts
150 g/5 oz. cooked king
    prawns/jumbo shrimp
12 rice paper wrappers, 16 cm/
    6 inches diameter
a handful of fresh mint leaves
a handful of fresh coriander/
    cilantro leaves
12 fresh chives

Dipping sauce
1 hot fresh red chilli/chile
1 fat garlic clove, roughly
    chopped
1 generous tablespoon palm
    sugar/jaggery or brown sugar
freshly squeezed juice of 1 lime
½ tablespoon fish sauce
½ tablespoon rice wine vinegar
1 tablespoon chopped salted
    peanuts

SERVES 4–6

Prepare the dipping sauce first. Remove the seeds from the chilli/chile and finely chop the flesh. Roughly chop the garlic and pound to a paste using a pestle and mortar. Add the remaining ingredients and mix until smooth. Taste and add more fish sauce or sugar to balance the flavours as necessary. Set aside while you prepare the rolls.

Have all the ingredients for the rolls lined up on a tray. Pour boiling water over the rice noodles in a bowl and let soak for 5 minutes. Cut the cucumber and carrot into fine matchsticks. Finely shred the lettuce and cut the prawns/shrimp in half lengthways to make them thinner. Drain the noodles well on paper towels.

Take one rice paper wrapper at a time and soak in a bowl of warm water for 1 minute, or until soft. Very gently lift it out of the water and drain quickly on a clean kitchen cloth. Lay the wrapper on the work surface, cut the noodles into short, equal lengths and arrange in a neat pile down the middle of the wrapper, leaving space at each end to fold the wrapper over later. Top with the shredded vegetables, the prawns/shrimp and arrange some of the herb leaves over the top. Fold one side of the wrapper over the length of the filling, then bring the short sides over to encase the ingredients. Tightly roll the wrapper up to form a neat cigar shape. Arrange on a plate, seam-side down.

Continue with the remaining wrappers and ingredients. Serve with the dipping sauce.

Mixed sashimi with ginger soy dressing and micro herbs

Although this recipe uses salmon and tuna, you can ask your fishmonger for the very best, freshest fish he has to offer for this pretty sashimi with ginger soy dressing and micro herb garnish. It is fine to sear the fish quickly in a smoking-hot frying pan, if you wish.

250 g/8 oz. sushi-grade tuna
    fillet
250 g/8 oz. skinless salmon
    fillet, pin bones removed
a 5-cm/2-inch piece of
    mooli/daikon radish
4 red-skinned radishes,
    trimmed
4 spring onions/scallions,
    trimmed
1 tablespoon pickled ginger
micro herbs, baby
    rocket/arugula or fresh
    coriander/cilantro

Ginger soy dressing
½ fresh red chilli/chile, finely
    chopped
½–1 teaspoon wasabi paste
2 tablespoons soy sauce
freshly squeezed juice
    of ½ lime

SERVES 4

Cut the fish into thin slices and arrange on a platter.

Peel and cut the mooli/daikon into fine matchsticks. Cut the radishes into fine matchsticks. Thinly slice the spring onions/scallions. Mix the mooli/daikon, radishes and spring onions/scallions together and add to the platter. Add the pickled ginger, too.

To make the ginger soy dressing, mix together the chopped chilli/chile, wasabi paste, soy sauce and lime juice in a little bowl.

Garnish the sashimi with the micro herbs and serve immediately with the ginger soy dressing.

Vegetarian dishes

In recent years the humble vegetable has taken an increasingly starring role in restaurant dishes. In this chapter you'll find deliciously different meat-free recipes that will enable you to cater for vegetarian friends and satisfy your non-veggie guests too.

Tomato basil granita

Granitas, with their distinctive rough texture, are gloriously refreshing treats. Sweet tomatoes and fragrant basil are a classic combination, which work well in this icy form. Serve this pretty pink granita as a refreshing summer appetizer.

700 g/1½ lbs. ripe tomatoes, scalded and peeled (see Tip on page 49)
100 g/½ cup caster/superfine sugar
freshly squeezed juice of ½ lemon
a handful of fresh basil leaves

SERVES 6

Put the peeled tomatoes to a food processor and blend to a purée. Add the sugar and lemon juice and blend again briefly. Shred the basil leaves and stir through the mixture.

Transfer the mixture to a freezerproof container, cover and freeze for 2 hours. Remove from the freezer and, using a fork, scrape the frozen part from around the edges of the container, mixing it in with the unfrozen part. Freeze for a further hour, then repeat the scraping and mixing process. Freeze for a further hour, stir and serve.

Tomato mousse

With its delicate flavour and smooth texture, this mousse makes an elegant and novel appetizer for a summer dinner party.

1 tablespoon olive oil
1 shallot, finely chopped
1 sprig of fresh thyme
800 g/1¾ lbs. tomatoes, scalded and peeled (see Tip on page 49)
1 roasted red (bell) pepper
6 sheets leaf gelatine, soaked and squeezed
200 ml/¾ cup double heavy cream
salt and freshly ground black pepper, to season
4 cherry tomatoes
8 fresh basil leaves, shredded

6 ramekins, lightly oiled

SERVES 6

Heat the oil in a heavy-bottomed saucepan set over a low heat. Add the shallot and thyme and cook until softened. Add the tomatoes, cover and cook for 5 minutes. Uncover and stir well to break down the tomatoes. Add the roasted (bell) pepper and cook for 5 minutes. Season well, blend to a purée and set aside to cool.

Heat a little of the cooled purée in a small pan set over a medium heat, until just below boiling point. Remove from the direct heat and stir in the soaked gelatine until melted. Mix the gelatine mixture into the purée and cool completely. Whip the cream in a large bowl to soft peaks. Gently fold in the cooled tomato purée. Divide the mixture between the prepared ramekins and chill in the fridge for around 4 hours, until set.

Halve, deseed and dice the cherry tomatoes and mix with the basil. Use to garnish each tomato mousse before serving at once.

Baked cheesecakes with salted honey walnuts

This twist on a classic baked cheesecake is ideal for a special occasion. Use your preferred strong-flavoured cheese in the recipe and seasonal herbs. Serve with a crisp green salad and slices of green apple on the side, if liked.

Crust
200 g/7 oz. oatcakes
50 g/3½ tablespoons butter
3 tablespoons honey
salt and freshly ground black pepper, to season

Filling
150 g/⅔ cup cream cheese
150 g/⅔ cup vegetarian ricotta cheese
75 ml/⅓ cup sour cream
1 teaspoon Dijon mustard
3 egg yolks
100 g/3½ oz. vegetarian cheese of your choice, such as Wensleydale, feta or any blue cheese
a few chives, scissored
3 egg whites
50 g/¾ cup finely grated Parmesan
salt and ground white pepper, to season

Salted honey walnuts
2 tablespoons honey
2 teaspoons brown sugar
2 teaspoons sea salt, plus extra for sprinkling
100 g/¾ cup walnut pieces

4 chefs' rings, greased

SERVES 4

Preheat the oven to 150°C (300°F) Gas 2.

To make the crust, put the oatcakes in a plastic food bag and crush them with a rolling pin, or whizz to crumbs in a food processor. Tip the crumbs into a large bowl and season with salt and pepper. Melt the butter over a gentle heat in a saucepan until the butter foams and turns golden. Remove from the heat and stir in the honey until dissolved. Combine the butter and honey with the oatcake crumbs. Press the crumbs into the bottom of the chefs' rings. Use the base of a glass to press down the mixture. Bake the crust in the preheated oven for 8–10 minutes until golden and firm.

Meanwhile, prepare the filling. Put the cream cheese, ricotta, sour cream, mustard and egg yolks in a bowl and whisk until light and fluffy. Crumble in the cheese, stir in the chives and season with salt and pepper.

In a separate bowl, and using clean beaters, beat the egg whites to medium peaks. Take a spoonful of the egg white and stir it through the cheese mixture to loosen it. Gently fold in the remaining egg whites with a metal spoon.

Cool the oven to 160°C (325°F) Gas 3. Spoon the mixture into the chefs' rings to cover the oatcake crust and sprinkle with the Parmesan. Bake in the preheated oven for 30–40 minutes, until the cheesecakes are golden on top and set but still have a slight, wobble when you gently shake the pans.

To make the salted honey walnuts, put the honey, sugar and salt in a pan. Dissolve over a low heat, stirring, until the sugar is dissolved and the honey has turned liquid. Remove from the heat, add the walnut pieces and stir until well coated. Turn the nuts onto the baking sheet and sprinkle with extra salt. Leave to cool and set.

Use a knife to loosen the edges of the cheesecakes and turn them out. Serve warm or at room temperature with the salted honey walnuts.

Mediterranean vegetable and feta pastries

Inspired by the popular Greek-style cheese pies, these light and crisp pastries incase a delicious filling of courgettes/zucchini, sun-dried tomatoes and tangy feta cheese. Serve hot with a simple lemon and garlic yogurt dip on the side.

100 g/7 tablespoons butter
1 packet of ready-made filo/phyllo pastry dough
2 tablespoons poppy seeds or sesame seeds (optional)

Filling
2 courgettes/zucchini, deseeded
120 g/1 cup sun-dried or sun-blush tomatoes
200 g/7 oz. feta cheese
finely grated zest of 1 lemon
1 garlic clove, crushed
½ teaspoon chilli/hot red pepper flakes
1 teaspoon mustard seeds
freshly ground nutmeg, to taste (optional)
salt and freshly ground black pepper, to season

Lemon and garlic yogurt dip
300 ml/about 1½ cups plain yogurt
grated zest and juice of 2 lemons
2 garlic cloves, crushed
salt and freshly ground black pepper, to season

a baking sheet, greased

MAKES 18

Preheat the oven to 190°C (375°F) Gas 5.

To make the filling, cube the courgette/zucchini and chop the sun-dried tomatoes. Put into a bowl, crumble in the feta and add the lemon zest, garlic, chilli/hot red pepper flakes, mustard seeds and nutmeg (if using). Combine well and season to taste with salt and pepper. Set aside until ready to fill the pastries.

To make the yogurt dip, combine the yogurt, lemon zest and garlic in a small bowl. Season to taste with lemon juice, salt and pepper.

Preheat oven to 200°C (400°F) Gas 6.

To make the pastries, melt the butter in a small saucepan set over low heat. Brush one sheet of filo/phyllo pastry dough with melted butter, then lay another pastry sheet on top. Lightly brush with butter. (Keep the remaining pastry well covered under a damp tea cloth until needed.) Put a tablespoon of filling at one end of the strip leaving a 1-cm/³⁄₈-inch gap at the bottom and on either side. Form the filling into a rough triangle, and fold the bottom excess up onto the filling. Roll the pastry up tightly, making the shape of the triangle.

Once the samosa is formed, brush with butter and sprinkle with poppy or sesame seeds, and put on the prepared baking sheet. Repeat with the remaining pastry until you have used all the pastry and filling.

Bake in the preheated oven for 10–12 minutes until the pastries are golden brown, and serve immediately, with the lemon and garlic yogurt dip on the side.

Vegetable tempura with nuoc cham sauce

Tempura batter gives these simply prepared vegetables a more interesting texture and appearance for little extra effort. Popular Vietnamese nuoc cham sauce is particularly good with this recipe and can also be drizzled over rice dishes.

1 large courgette/zucchini, core and seeds removed, flesh cut into strips

1 large aubergine/eggplant, cut into rings

500 ml/2 cups vegetable oil, for frying

40 g/⅓ cup plain/all-purpose flour

60 g/½ cup plus 1½ tablespoons cornflour/ cornstarch

¼ teaspoon baking powder

100–150 ml/⅓–⅔ cup iced sparkling water

a pinch of salt

½ head of cauliflower, cut into bite-size florets

½ head of broccoli, cut into bite-size florets

3 red (bell) peppers, deseeded and cut into strips

Nuoc cham sauce

1 small lime

3 garlic cloves, crushed

2 small hot green chillies/chiles, deseeded and thinly sliced

4 teaspoons raw cane sugar

60 ml/¼ cup Vietnamese- style fish sauce (or vegetarian substitution such as tamari)

SERVES 4–6

For best results, place the courgette/zucchini and aubergine/eggplant in a sieve/strainer and sprinkle all over with table salt, then leave for 10 minutes; you will notice liquid has leached out of the vegetables. Rinse well in water to remove the salt and pat dry with paper towels.

To make the nuoc cham sauce, squeeze the juice from the lime into a small bowl and set aside. Scrape the pulp from the lime and grind it, along with the garlic and chillies, with a pestle and mortar to form a paste. If you find it difficult to get a paste, the ingredients could be briefly pulsed in a food processor. Add 75 ml/⅓ of cup water and the sugar to the bowl of lime juice and stir until the sugar has dissolved. Scrape the paste into the bowl, add the fish sauce (or tamari) and mix well.

When you are ready to cook the tempura vegetables, set your deep-fat fryer to 190°C (375°F), or fill a wide deep saucepan ⅓ full with vegetable oil and set over a medium heat.

Make the batter immediately before cooking. Combine the flour, cornflour/cornstarch and baking powder in a bowl. Add the water to the flour mixture, whisking to combine quickly, but stop as soon as the liquid is combined – the odd lump is okay, and better than over-working the batter. The consistency should be slightly looser than a crêpe batter – a light coating batter is what you want, not one that is thick and gloopy. The batter also must be ice cold, so drop an ice cube in the batter to keep it chilled while using.

As soon as the oil has come to temperature, make sure the vegetables are dry and then dip them in the batter, shake off any excess and put them into the hot oil using a slotted metal spoon. Cook for 1–2 minutes until pale golden (tempura does not colour like other batter so do not wait for a deep colour). Repeat, cooking in small batches as cooking too much at the same time can reduce the oil temperature. Drain on paper towels and lightly sprinkle with salt. Serve immediately with the nuoc cham for dipping.

Pot-sticker dumplings with Chinese dipping sauce

Not to be confused with wontons, pot-stickers, as they are called in North America, are a form of Chinese dumpling that is fried, steamed and then fried again so they are at once both soft and crispy.

125 g/2 cups finely chopped Chinese cabbage

1 teaspoon salt

1 leek, trimmed and finely chopped

2 garlic cloves, crushed

2 tablespoons freshly chopped coriander/cilantro

250 g/1 cup firm smoked tofu

24 gyoza wrappers

2 tablespoons vegetable oil

garlic chive flowers, to garnish (optional)

Chinese dipping sauce

50 ml/¼ cup light soy sauce

2 teaspoons Chinese black vinegar

1 teaspoon caster/granulated sugar

1 teaspoon freshly grated root ginger

1 teaspoon sesame oil

¼ teaspoon chilli/chile oil

a baking sheet lined with baking parchment

SERVES 4

Put the cabbage in a large mixing bowl with the salt and toss well to coat. Transfer to a colander and leave to drain for 1 hour to remove as much water as possible from the cabbage. Squeeze out any remaining water and put the cabbage in a clean large mixing bowl with the leek, garlic and coriander/cilantro. Crumble in the tofu and mix in until combined.

Working one at a time, lay the gyoza wrappers out flat and place a teaspoon of the tofu mixture on one half of each wrapper. Dampen the edges with a little cold water, fold the wrapper over the filling and carefully press the edges together to seal.

Preheat the oven to 110°C (225°F) Gas ¼ (or the lowest heat setting). Heat 1 tablespoon of the oil in a wok or large non-stick frying pan/skillet set over a high heat. Add half the dumplings and fry for about 1 minute until the bottoms are golden. Add 100 ml/⅓ cup of water and simmer, partially covered, for 5 minutes, until the water has evaporated. Cook for a further 2–3 minutes until the bottoms are crispy. Transfer the dumplings to the prepared baking sheet, turn off the oven and set in the still-warm oven while you cook the remaining dumplings in the same way.

To make the dipping sauce, whisk all the ingredients together in a bowl, or, if you have a clean glass jar with a lid, put all the ingredients into the jar, screw on the lid and shake well.

Arrange the dumplings on plates and serve drizzled with the dipping sauce. Garnish with garlic chive flowers, if wished, and serve.

Lemon and wild rice stuffed fennel with fresh tomato sauce

This light and fragrant dish contains fresh herbs, fennel and lemon and is served with a light tomato sauce. It can be made ahead of time, then simply finished in the oven – perfect for dining al fresco in summer.

8 fennel bulbs

1 tablespoon olive oil, plus extra for drizzling

4 tablespoons white wine

100 g/²/3 cup wild rice

400 ml/³/4 cup vegetable stock

1 shallot, chopped

2 garlic cloves, crushed

grated zest and freshly squeezed juice of ½ lemon

60 g/scant 1 cup grated Parmesan

a handful chopped fresh flat-leaf parsley

60 g/1 cup soft breadcrumbs (or ½–¾ cup dried)

salt and freshly ground black pepper, to season

Fresh tomato sauce

4 ripe vine tomatoes

2 shallots, finely chopped

1 garlic clove, crushed

2 tablespoons olive oil

1 tablespoon white wine

1 teaspoon white sugar

1 teaspoon tomato purée/paste

freshly squeezed lemon juice

1 teaspoon balsamic vinegar

a handful of chopped fresh flat-leaf parsley leaves

SERVES 4

Preheat the oven to 180°C (350°F) Gas 4.

To prepare the fennel, cut a thin slice off the bottom of each fennel bulb so that it sits flat. Cut about 2 cm/¾ inch off the top of each bulb, so that you can get to the centre. Hollow the flesh out of each bulb's centre and finely chop it. Set aside and reserve. Put a large sheet of kitchen foil on a baking sheet (sufficient to wrap the fennel bulbs), and arrange the fennel bulbs on it. Season with salt and pepper, drizzle with olive oil, pour over half the wine, then seal the parcel. Bake in the preheated oven for about 40 minutes, until the fennel is soft.

Meanwhile, make the tomato sauce. Blanch the tomatoes in boiling water for 10 seconds to remove the skins. Deseed, then finely chop the flesh and set aside. Put the shallots in a saucepan, add the garlic and cook over a low heat for 2 minutes. Add the olive oil and the wine. Add the tomato flesh and simmer for 5 minutes. Add the sugar, tomato purée/paste and lemon juice. Stir in the vinegar and herbs. Add a litte water to the sauce to thin, if needed. Set aside.

To prepare the filling, put the wild rice in a saucepan with the vegetable stock and cook according to the packet instructions. Meanwhile, heat 1 tablespoon of the olive oil in a frying pan/skillet. Add the shallot and cook over low heat for 5–10 minutes until softened but not coloured. Add the reserved chopped fennel flesh, garlic, lemon zest and juice, the remaining wine and season well with salt and pepper. Cover and simmer over a low heat until the fennel is soft and golden and the liquid has evaporated. Add the cooked wild rice, half the Parmesan cheese and parsley to the pan and season well with salt and pepper.

Fill each of the fennel bulbs with the wild rice mixture and top with the breadcrumbs, remaining Parmesan and reserved parsley. Serve warm with the tomato sauce on the side.

Arancini with pecorino cheese, porcini mushrooms and melting mozzarella

You can use leftover risotto for these rice balls if you happen to have any, but as they are so delicious it's worth making the risotto especially. They can be prepared and rolled in advance; coat them in breadcrumbs and fry just before serving.

15 g/½ oz. dried porcini mushrooms

1 tablespoon olive oil

2 tablespoons unsalted butter

2 shallots, finely chopped

1 garlic clove, crushed

250 g/1¼ cups risotto rice (arborio or carnaroli)

750–850 ml/3–3½ cups hot vegetable stock

40 g/⅓ cup grated Pecorino

1 tablespoon freshly chopped flat-leaf parsley or oregano

125 g/4 oz. mozzarella cheese, diced

100 g/¾ cup plain/ all-purpose flour

2 eggs, lightly beaten

200 g/2 cups fresh, fine breadcrumbs

about 1 litre/4 cups sunflower oil, for frying

salt and freshly ground black pepper, to season

MAKES 15–18

Soak the porcini mushrooms in a small bowl of boiling water for about 15 minutes, or until soft. Drain well on paper towels and finely chop.

Heat the olive oil and butter in a medium saucepan and add the shallots, garlic and chopped porcini. Cook over a low–medium heat until soft but not coloured. Add the rice to the pan and stir to coat well in the buttery mixture. Gradually add the vegetable stock 1 ladleful at a time and as the stock is absorbed by the rice, add another ladleful, stirring continuously as you do so. Continue cooking in this way until the rice is al dente and the stock is used up. Remove the pan from the heat, add the pecorino and herbs, and season well with salt and black pepper. Tip the risotto into a bowl and let cool completely.

Once the rice is cold, divide it into walnut-size pieces and roll into balls. Taking one ball at a time, flatten it into a disc in the palm of your hand, press some diced mozzarella in the middle and wrap the rice around it to completely encase the cheese. Shape into a neat ball. Repeat with the remaining risotto.

Tip the flour, beaten eggs and breadcrumbs into separate shallow bowls. Roll the rice balls first in the flour, then coat well in the eggs and finally, roll them in the breadcrumbs to completely coat.

Fill your deep-fat fryer with sunflower oil or pour oil to a depth of about 5 cm/2 inches into a deep saucepan. Heat until a cube of bread sizzles and browns in about 5 seconds. Cook the arancini, in batches, in the hot oil for 3–4 minutes or until crisp, hot and golden brown. Drain on paper towels and serve immediately.

Sharing plates and boards

Modern entertaining doesn't have to be formal. A well thought out plate to share is the ideal solution for fuss-free midweek entertaining and drinks parties. Simply select and arrange a delicious selection of charcuterie, seafood, crudités or cheese and let the wine and conversation flow.

French charcuterie board

With some clever shopping and a few good recipes you can easily put together a spread of delicious French cured meats and pâtés that makes an indulgent sharing board. Lay out your food artfully on a wooden board to create a rustic feel and serve with cornichons, radishes, black olive tapenade and plenty of freshly baked baguette.

To buy in
a selection of charcuterie including Bayonne ham and saucisson sec (cured sausage)
black olive tapenade
pickled cornichons (baby gherkins)
French wholegrain mustard
radishes
good-quality freshly baked baguette/French stick

To cook (optional)
Pork rillettes (see page 76)
Pâté de Campagne (see page 75)

To drink
French white wine such as Sancerre
dry French rosé wine
French sparkling white wine such as Champagne or Crémant d'Alsace
French red wine such as Pinot Noir, serve slightly chilled
citron pressé (lemonade)

Shopping well is key here. There is a wide variety of French hams (jambon) to choose from. Some are raw and air-cured (jambon cru), and others are smoked or cooked. Look for regional varieties marked Protected Geographical Indication (PGI), which ensures products are genuine.

The most ubiquitous PGI ham is Jambon sec – a dry-cured ham which has been dry-cured for at least 3 months (pictured opposite). Hams in this category include those produced in the Ardennes, Auvergne, Bayonne, Lacaune, Najac and Savoie regions. Jambon sec superiéur is a variation that comes from pigs raised by traditional methods, such as Bigorre ham from free-range Gascony black pigs raised in the Pyrénnées mountains. Jambon de Bayonne is a particular speciality of the Pays Basque region in South-west France and is prized for its rich, nutty flavour. It comes from pigs that enjoy a 'clean' diet, which includes chestnuts, acorns and beechnuts. The hind leg meat is salted (with local Salies-de-Béarn salt), then air-dried and matured for up to 10 months.

Jambon d'Ardenne is produced in North-eastern France and has long been renowned the world over for its texture and very mild, slightly sweet flavour. This is not to be confused with Ardenne Ham, which is salted and air-dried for several months and has a fine, dry texture. This ham is produced in Belgium.

Saucisson sec is a dry-cured sausage (pictured opposite). Much like Italian Salami in style, it uses minced/ground meat seasoned with fresh garlic, black peppercorns and sea salt. It is hand-tied and cured for 30 days.

You could buy in a good pâté but if you want to impress, try the recipes for pork rillettes and/or the pâté de Campagne. Rillettes are similar to pâté but slow-cooked and don't traditionally contain liver. Their texture is rougher, more like shredded meat, and they are often spooned, rather than spread, onto a slice of crusty baguette. Terrines (or pâtés au terrine) are also similar to pâtés but made with more coarsely chopped ingredients, baked in a loaf mould and served in slices.

Italian antipasti board

Some of the best-known cured meat products available around the world are of Italian origin. Take full advantage of your nearest Italian grocer to source a selection of prosciutto and bresaola, arrange your bounty artfully on a wooden board or ceramic platter and serve with generous glasses of red wine.

To buy in
a selection of cured and sliced Italian salumi, including Parma ham, prosciutto, salami and bresaola
sun-blushed/semi-dried tomatoes in oil
Italian olives (bright green Sicilian Nocellara or black Cerignola from Puglia)
grissini (breadsticks), or make our own (see below)
Parmesan or pecorino cheese
extra-virgin olive oil and aged balsamic vinegar

To cook (optional)
Cherry Tomato Bruschetta (see page 20)
Arancini (see page 126)
Breadsticks (see page 34)

To drink
Prosecco
Italian white wine such as Pinot Grigio
Italian red wine such as Chianti or Montepulciano or a chilled Valpolicella
Italian beer, such as Peroni Nastro Azzurro
San Pellegrino sparkling water

Prosciutto crudo is perhaps the most common cured product where the meat isn't minced/ground, the most famous type being from Parma ('Parma ham' or prosciutto di Parma, pictured opposite). This is a whole hind leg of the pig, which is dry-cured in salt and then hung for up to a year (sometimes longer). The meat often comes from more mature pigs than for fresh pork products; fresh pork and sausages tend to come from pigs under 4 months old, whereas most forms of prosciutto require the animal to be at least 6 months old. *Coppa* or *capocollo* is a cured pork neck that is sliced like prosciutto (pictured opposite).

Salami is probably the best known 'comminuted' (minced/ground) cured meat, and popular regional varieties include Milano and Napoli (pictured opposite). The process involves mincing/grinding the meat and combining it with seasoning and herbs, stuffing the mixture into a casing and air-drying it. *Mortadella* is 'the light pink' one but don't make the mistake of imagining it tastes anything like pork luncheon meat – the colour is comparable but that's it. The minced/ ground pork is puréed so that it is very smooth. It is often mixed with pistachios as well as the seasoning and salts, and it's hung in a casing, like salami.

Bresaola is one of the best cured beefs from Italy and originates from the Lombardy region in the North. It is a dry-salted, lean cut of beef that is air-dried. *Pastrami* is usually made with brisket or topside/top round. It is salted, spiced and dry-cured.

Light and fruity wines are good with the bold flavours of Italian cured meats. You don't want to overpower the flavour of the ham. Good tipples to serve with any Italian selection are chilled Prosecco or crisp Pinot Grigio. Alternatively, go for a full-bodied Chianti or Montepulciano d'Abruzzo. You can also try a lightly chilled red wine, such as a Valpolicella. On a hot day, an ice-cold Italian beer, such as Peroni Nastro Azzurro, works well too.

Spanish tapas board

Tapas is the tradition of serving little dishes of food with drinks. Traditional tapas bites include hams and chorizo, but add some olives, almonds and hot bites served on cocktails sticks, and you have a vibrant feast that can be enjoyed with little glasses of chilled Spanish fino sherry.

To buy in
a selection of cured and sliced Spanish meats (carnes curadas), including Chorizo and hams
Spanish manzanilla and Sevillano (queen) olives
roasted red (bell) peppers in olive oil
Manchego cheese
salted Marcona almonds

To cook (optional)
Frittata Bites (see page 10)
Chorizo and Scallop Skewers (see page 27)

To drink
Fino sherry
Spanish red wine such as Rioja, Tempranillo or Garnacha
dry and crisp Spanish rosé wine, such as one from Navarra
Cava
Spanish beer, such as San Miguel
Casera (sparkling lemon soda)

The best-known Spanish cured meat is, without doubt, chorizo. This is made from minced/ground and seasoned pork, which gains its a lovely smoky flavour from paprika and chilli/chili. The mix is stuffed into a casing and hung to air-dry. It can be eaten as it is and is also very adaptable for cooked recipes – perhaps even more so than salami, because it contains slightly more oil.

Jamón Serrano (literally 'ham from the mountains') is whole cured ham, similar to prosciutto, and is usually served in thin slices. It has a lovely rich, dark flavour and comes from regions all over Spain. Jamón Ibérico is a protected origin variety of Spanish cured ham (pictured opposite). *Jamón Ibérico de Bellota* is one of the most expensive meat products in the world. The pigs – usually Landrace breed – traditionally live to 2 years old and roam free in forests. For the last few months of their lives, they gorge happily on acorns, which adds around 20 per cent more fat to them. It's rich, delicious and expensive. Chorizo *Ibérico de Bellota* is also popular and pricey; made from the comminuted (see page 133) shoulder and neck meat from those acorn-guzzling Iberian pigs (pictured opposite).

Cecina de León is a hind-leg of cured beef from the León region of Spain. The Spanish Cecina meat range occasionally uses horse- and goat-meat as well, however it is always produced by a dry salt-cure and hanging process. When sliced, it is a vibrant shade of maroon.

Serve your meats with a selection of Spanish nibbles, include salted Marcona almonds, marinated olives, slices of salty Manchego cheese and roasted red (bell) peppers (*pimentos rojos asados*) and wash down with small glasses of chilled fino sherry, your choice of wine or even an ice-cold Spanish beer.

French seafood feast 'plateau de fruits de mer'

Seafood lovers will be thrilled with this luxurious treat. A firm favourite in Parisian brasseries, where diners relish enormous seafood platters washed down with bottles of chilled Muscadet or Champagne. Plenty of crushed ice is key to impressive presentation and provide your guests specialist tools, finger bowls and napkins.

To buy in
a selection of fresh, prepared
*   seafood, such as lobster,*
*   crab, prawns/shrimp,*
*   oysters, mussels and clams*
fresh mayonnaise and
*   seafood cocktail sauce*
lemon wedges, for squeezing
fresh flat-leaf parsley,
*   to garnish*
French sourdough baguette
*   such as Pain au Levain*
pots of unsalted French butter

To cook (optional)
Lobster Bisque (see page 45),
*   served in small coffee cups*
*   ahead of the feast*
Shallot Vinegar (see right)

To drink
Champagne
French white wine, such
*   as Muscadet or Chablis*
Perrier sparkling water

Choose a selection of the freshest seafood you can find and ask your fishmonger to do the work for you. Include crab claws and or legs, lobster or langoustines and some large shell-on *crevettes* (prawns/shrimp) – ideally more than one variety. *Huitres* (oysters) are the dominate feature of most French seafood platters so do include these if you think your guests will enjoy them. You will frequently find *moules* (mussels) served at more casual French restaurants and bistros (more traditionally with French fries as the dish *moules-frites*) and these make a good addition here too and can be substituted for the oysters. To create a lovely visual display as well as an array of flavours, you should also include a selection of smaller shellfish, such as winkles, whelks and cockles. The French word for clams is the same as in English, but you may also see varieties of them called *praires* or *palourdes*. In a good French seafood restaurant you might also be served rather more exotic fare, including *oursins* (sea urchins) and *bigorneaux* or *bulots* (sea snails) so if you have access to them, why not wow your guess and include these too!

The shellfish should all be cooked and chilled before serving on a bed of ice, ideally in a shallow metal bowl or platter. Shells should be opened before serving so that extracting the flesh isn't too arduous for your guests but have some tools to hand just in case. Put out a lobster cracker (which allows you to crack open shells without crushing it into tiny bits), a three-pronged oyster fork and long, two-pronged seafood forks.

Serve with plenty of fresh baguette, lemon wedges for squeezing and a selection of condiments, including mayonnaise and shallot vinegar. To make this, simply peel and finely dice two shallots and put them in a bowl. Cover with 125 ml/$^1/_2$ cup red wine vinegar and whisk with a fork. Season with salt and pepper. This will keep for up to 2 days, if refrigerated.

Enjoy your luxury feast with plenty of cold Champagne or a well-chilled French white wine – a Muscadet or Chablis is ideal.

Provençal crudités platter 'le grand aïoli'

This extravaganza originates from Provence in the South of France and is a glorious celebration of the region's produce. It is a colourful selection of tender young vegetables, displayed on a platter and served with a thick garlicky mayonnaise called aïoli, which is often referred to as 'the butter of Provence'. This makes a great vegetarian centrepiece for any buffet or a summer appetizer for sharing.

To buy in
a selection of raw or blanched baby vegetables, to include (bell) peppers, carrots, radishes, cucumber, spring onions/scallions, fennel, celery hearts, sugar snap peas or mangetout/snow peas, fine green beans and cherry tomatoes
anchoïade (anchovy dip)
organic eggs, hard-boiled/hard-cooked, peeled and halved
French country bread, ideally a Provençal 'fougasse'
sea salt flakes
pots of unsalted French butter

To cook (optional)
Saffron and Garlic Aïoli (see right)
Lebanese Houmous (see page 31)
Majorcan Gazpacho, served in shot glasses (see page 49)

To drink
crisp dry French rosé wine, ideally from Provence
crisp white wine such as Sauvignon Blanc or unwooded Chardonnay
citron pressé (lemonade)

Traditionally, 'Le Grand Aïoli' comprises of a selection of raw or blanched baby vegetables and hard-boiled/hard-cooked eggs that are served with a rich, garlicky sauce for dipping – the aïoli which gives this feast its name. Arrange the prepared vegetables on a large oval platter and serve the dip in a bowl, then let your guests help themselves.

A good selection of *crudités* should include red or yellow (bell) peppers cut into strips, baby carrots with the tops left on (or larger carrots cut into batons), radishes with stems and leaves on, cucumber (unpeeled and sliced into thick batons lengthways), trimmed spring onions/scallions, fennel (quartered and sliced), celery hearts with the leaves left on, sugar snap peas or mangetout/snowpeas, fine green beans (blanched) and some sweet cherry tomatoes on the vine.

Serve your vegetable platter with hard-boiled/hard-cooked eggs, plenty of French country bread, ideally a Provençal *fougasse* or 'ladder bread' and a simple Saffron and Garlic Aïoli. Make this by putting room-temperature egg yolks (organic and very fresh) in a bowl and add 1 teaspoon Dijon mustard, 1 teaspoon crushed saffron threads (soaked in 1 tablespoon lukewarm water), 1 crushed garlic clove and ½ teaspoon each of salt and black pepper. While whisking, slowly drizzle in 200 ml/¾ cup grapeseed oil until it is all incorporated. Add 1 tablespoon freshly squeezed lemon juice and mix again to finish. Cover and keep refrigerated until ready to serve.

To drink, opt for a Provençal rosé wine, well chilled or, if preferred, a light white, such as an unwooded Chardonnay or Sauvignon Blanc.

Seasonal cheeseboard

Cheeseboards are simple to assemble and always popular. A specialist cheesemonger is the ideal place to shop, but most supermarkets now carry a good range. Offer attractive accompaniments that reflect the season and serve with good biscuits/crackers and bread. Present your treasure on a wooden board, wicker tray or slate.

To buy in
a selection of 5–7 cheeses of varying colours, flavours and textures
fresh or dried fruits, depending on the season
membrillo (Spanish quince preserve) or damson paste
spiced fruit chutneys and preserves
a selection of cheese biscuits/crackers, including water biscuits and oatcakes
some enriched breads (such as walnut and raisin bread), optional

To cook (optional)
Bacon Bites (see page 137)
Curry Cashew Crunch Cookies (see page 138)

To drink
an aged or Porty red wine such as Rioja, Côte du Rhone or Zinfandel
a fruity red wine such as Merlot, Chilean Pinot Noir, or with soft goat's cheese, try a Sauvignon Blanc
artisanal ciders
craft beers

Choose a selection of cheeses with flavours ranging from creamy through to piquant, and a variety of textures too: velvet-soft goat's cheese, gooey Camembert, a sharp blue cheese, a firm Comté and an aged Cheddar, for example.

You might like to start with a Gorgonzola or other soft blue cheese, a firm goat's cheese, such as *Crottin de Chavignol*, a wedge of Brie, a whole camembert (still packaged in it's attractive round wooden box), a French Comté or similar dense Swiss cheese such as Gruyère. A Spanish Manchego can be a good edition, and look out for aged or smoked varieties or a good mature/sharp Cheddar.

Different cheeses are complemented by both fresh and dried fruits, so offer these alongside. In spring green apple slices, fresh herbs and baby salad leaves can be appealing, while in summer fresh cherries and grapes work well, as do fresh figs. Come autumn/fall pears and red apples come into their own and in winter dried apricots, figs, Medjool dates and large Muscat raisins all work well. Shell-on nuts are both delicious and attractive to look at on our board, especially on a festive occasion. Walnuts work particularly well with blue cheeses, salted almonds with hard cheeses such as Manchego and hazelnuts with smoked cheeses. Preserves are also a nice addition. Choose a fruit paste such as the Spanish quince membrillo or damson paste, or jarred preserves such as spiced apple or pear chutneys or caramelized onions, which work particuly well with gooey French cheeses such as Camembert.

Arrange your cheeses artfully and garnish with fresh or dried fruit and nuts, according to the season. Let the weather guide you on drinks too. Red wine is an obvious choice, but don't be afraid to experiment. A chilled Sauvignon Blanc works very well with a goat's cheese in summer and good artisanal ciders and craft beers can also pair very well with an autumn/fall board. The key is to experiment and find matches that you enjoy first and then share them with your friends.

Index

Recipe credits

Miranda Ballard
Chicken liver pâté
Chorizo and scallop skewers
Devils on Horseback
French charcuterie board
Horses on Devilback
Hot prosciutto parcels stuffed with goat's cheese and fresh basil
Italian antipasti board
Parma ham & grapefruit
Parma ham & melon
Pâté de campagne
Pork rillettes
Prosciutto, artichoke, fig & Roquefort salad
Spanish tapas board

Jenny Linford
Cherry tomato & basil bruschetta
Green tomato & sorrel soup
Smoked mackerel cherry tomatoes
Tomato basil granita
Tomato blinis
Tomato mousse
Plum tomato tartlets
Melon, tomato & feta salad
Tuna empañadas

Chloe Coker and Jane Montgomery
Asian-style hot & sour salad with marinated tofu
Individual baked cheesecakes with salted honey walnuts
Lemon & wild rice stuffed fennel with fresh tomato sauce
Roasted aubergine/eggplant & red onion dip with paprika pitta crisps
Roasted vegetable salad with grilled halloumi & basil oil
Summer vegetable carpaccio
Sweet potato houmous with breadsticks
Mediterranean vegetable and feta pastries

Vicky Jones
Black lentil pancakes with mint raita
Brazilian black-eyed bean & prawn/shrimp fritters
Chickpea, egg & potato salad
Greek fava dip
Lebanese houmous
Quinoa & butter bean salad with avocado
Shallot & banana bhajis

Belinda Williams
Chilled cucumber yogurt soup with red chilli/chile & mint salsa

Chilled smoked salmon, avocado & chive soup
Cream of celeriac & white bean soup with toasted hazelnuts
Fennel & courgette/zucchini soup with crème fraiche and Parmesan
Lobster bisque
Majorcan gazpacho

Shelagh Ryan
Chorizo, red (bell) pepper & pea frittata bites
Mini corn fritters with smoked salmon & lemon cream
Lamb koftes with a tahini yogurt dip
Salt & pepper squid with lime aioli
Thai fishcakes with nahm jim sauce

Dan May
Butternut squash & coconut milk soup
Chilli/chile-marinated salmon gravadlax
Jalapeño poppers
Vegetable tempura with nuoc cham

Annie Rigg
Arancini with pecorino, porcini & melting mozzarella
Mixed sashimi
Seafood cocktails
Vietnamese rice paper rolls

Valerie Aikman-Smith
Chicken tikka bites with Madras mango relish
Beef empañadas with Texan hot sauce
West Coast crab cakes

Liz Franklin
Bacon bites
Curry cashew crunch cookies

Maxine Clark
Crab empañadas
Scallop & black pudding puffs

Tori Haschka
Spicy coconut ceviche
Steak tartare with mustard cheese toasts

Jennifer Joyce
French seafood feast
Seasonal cheeseboard
Provençal crudités platter

Louise Pickford
Potsticker dumplings with Chinese dipping sauce

Picture credits

Steve Baxter
88 left, 89 left, 91, 108, 111, 112 below, 126–127

Peter Cassidy
8 above, below and left, 9 left, 12–16, 20–21, 40 above, 42, 43, 56, 59, 87, 99, 101, 106, 112 above and left, 115, 120, 128 above, 129, 136–140

Richard Jung
90

Erin Kunkel
9 right, 29, 71 right, 82, 88 below, 100

William Lingwood
28

Diana Miller
4 left

Steve Painter
25, 26, 40 left, right and below, 41 right, 44–49, 51–55, 67, 70 left and right, 71 left, 72–77, 81, 85, 88 right, 95, 103, 128 below, 131–135

William Reavell
1, 8 right, 22–23, 30–35, 41 left, 57, 60–64, 68, 104, 110, 112 right, 113 left, 116, 119, 124

Debi Treloar
17, 58 left, 69, 84, 144

Ian Wallace
5, 6, 109, 113 right, 123

Kate Whitaker
2, 3, 4 right, 10–11, 18, 27, 36–39, 50, 58 right, 65, 70 below, 78, 88 above, 92, 96

Isobel Wield
17, 58 left, 69, 84, 144

Ian Wallace
70 above, 86, 89 right, 107